D1442067

FACTS AT YOUR FINGERTIPS

ANCIENT AZTEC AND MAYA

BROWN
BEAR
BOOKS

Published by Brown Bear Books Limited

An imprint of:
The Brown Reference Group Ltd
68 Topstone Road
Redding
Connecticut 06896
USA

www.brownreference.com

ISBN-13 978-1-933834-58-0

Editorial Director: Lindsey Lowe
Managing Editor: Tim Cooke
Design Manager: David Poole
Designer: Sarah Williams
Picture Manager: Sophie Mortimer
Picture Researcher: Sean Hannaway
Text Editor: Anita Dalal
Indexer: Indexing Specialists (UK) Ltd

Printed in the United States of America

CONTENTS

INTRODUCTION

Early Peoples

This book is about Ancient America. Although people often talk of Christopher Columbus "discovering" America in 1492, prehistoric hunters had crossed into northwest America from Asia thousands of years earlier. By the time Columbus arrived, there were millions of Native Americans. Columbus called the people Indians, because he thought that he had traveled around the world and had landed in the East Indies. This book uses the term Native Americans, although some tribes are still commonly referred to as Indians, for example Plains and Natchez Indians.

There were—and still are—many Native American peoples, speaking separate languages and living in very different ways. In this book you will read about the most important peoples who lived in North, Central, and South America in the period from the end of the Ice Age to the beginning of European exploration and conquest in the late 15th century. Over these 12,000 years, each group of ancient Americans developed skills and traditions best suited to their environment and its resources. Many were nomadic hunters and gatherers of wild plants. A number were farmers who lived in well-organized towns and villages. Some were skilled craftsmen, producing fine pottery or textiles or working in precious metals. Others built great cities and ruled vast empires.

How do we learn about these peoples of ancient America and their ways of life? Some of them, like the Maya and the Aztec, used picture-writing to record important events, and we can still interpret it. But the majority had no form of writing at all. For the most part, therefore, modern knowledge depends upon archaeological evidence, but this also varies greatly. Some ancient Americans are well represented by the remains of their stone buildings, carvings, textiles, pottery, and metalwork. Others, like the nomadic hunters who lived in skin tents or brushwood shelters, have left little trace behind.

Ancient Aztec and Maya begins with an overview of the early history of the American continent. Then the book is divided into two main sections. The first looks in detail at the people, places, and history of North America. The second deals with Mesoamerica and South America, and in particular with the great civilizations such as those of the Aztec and Maya in Mexico and the Inca in Peru.

The account of ancient American history begins in detail around 1500 BCE. Two terms that are used may need explanation. "Latin America" means those areas where European languages derived from Latin (such as Spanish and Portuguese) are now spoken. "Mesoamerica" refers to those parts of Mexico and Central America (from Guatemala to Panama) that had advanced cultures before the Spanish Conquest.

This book is an atlas. The maps help you understand what was happening in different parts of America at different times. Many of the maps are accompanied by charts giving important dates or useful information. Throughout the book, there are also special spreads that focus on specific archaeological sites. They explain where the site is, what it was, what has been found there, and its significance to the people who created it.

Abbreviations used in this book

BCE = Before Common Era (also known as BC).
CE = Common Era (also known as AD).
c. = circa (about).
in = inch; ft = foot; yd = yard; mi = mile; cu = cubic.
cm = centimeter; m = meter; km = kilometer.

Ancient buildings of the Pueblo shelter under a cliff in Canyon de Chelly, Arizona; they were built in the 11th century CE, but were abandoned in about 1275 CE for reasons that remain unknown.

TIMELINE

	1200 BCE	1000 BCE	800 BCE	500 BCE	100 BCE
NORTH AMERICA	Poverty Point built c.1500.	End of Archaic period c.1200–1000.	Dorset people begin to spread over eastern Arctic c.1000.	Adena people in Ohio valley c.700.	Large villages such as Ipiutak built in Alaska c.500. Woodlands farmers move westward into Plains c.250.	Hopewell peop Ohio valley c Southwestern f (Hohokam, M Anasazi) c.10

Stone spearhead from Folsom, New Mexico, c.9000 BCE.

Clay figurine from Poverty Point, c.1500 BCE.

Ivory snow goggles and boss from Ipiutak, Alaska, c.500 BCE–500 CE.

	1200 BCE	1000 BCE	800 BCE	500 BCE	100 BCE
MESOAMERICA	Development of Olmec civilization. San Lorenzo founded c.1500.		Olmec site of La Venta founded c.900.		Decline of Olmec civilization c.400. Development of early Maya civilization c.300.	

Carving of trophy head from Cerro Sechin, Peru, c.1300 BCE.

Bowl from Tlapacoya, valley of Mexico, c.1200–900 BCE.

Olmec head, La c.900–400 BCE.

	1200 BCE	1000 BCE	800 BCE	500 BCE	100 BCE
SOUTH AMERICA	Oldest known metalwork c.1500.	Development of Chavín civilization c.1200.	Chavín de Huantar founded c.850.	Paracas tombs c.700–200.	Nazca people on south coast of Peru c.370 BCE–450 CE. Decline of Chavín de Huantar c.200.	Arawak India arrive in Ar c.100.

Thule people appear in Alaska c.500.

Cahokia founded c.600.

Mississippi towns built c.800.

Farming villages in eastern Plains.

Chaco Canyon towns built c.900–1100.

Northern Iroquoians settle around Great Lakes c.1000.

Thule people begin to spread over eastern Arctic c.1000.

Norse settlement in Newfoundland c.1000.

Cliff dwellings at Mesa Verde and Canyon de Chelly c.1100.

Drought in Southwest 1276–99.

Cliff dwellings abandoned c.1300.

Decline of Cahokia c.1450.

Cartier explores St. Lawrence valley 1535–36.

De Soto explores Southeast 1539–42.

Coronado explores Southwest and southern Plains 1540–42.

...and, Hopewell ..., 100 BCE–600 CE.

Stone paint palette from Snaketown, c.100–500 CE.

Kneeling cat figure from Key Marco, Florida, c.800–1500 CE.

Cliff Palace, Mesa Verde, c.1100 CE.

Teotihuacán founded c.150.

Development of Classic Maya civilization c.300.

Reign of Pacal at Palenque 618–53.

Teotihuacán destroyed c.750.

Collapse of lowland Maya civilization c.900.

Toltec city of Tula founded c.950.

Tula destroyed 1168.

Decline of Maya civilization in Yucatán c.1200.

Aztec city of Tenochtitlán founded c.1345.

Aztecs control valley of Mexico 1428.

Aztec empire reaches greatest extent 1502.

Cortés invades Mexico 1519.

Spaniards conquer Mexico and destroy Aztec empire 1519–21.

Clay house model, Ecuador, c.500 BCE–500 CE.

Moche pot c.100–500 CE.

Lord Chac Zutz from Palenque, 730 CE.

Inca silver statuette, c.1400–1520 CE.

...eople on ...oast of Peru ...0.

Development of Tiahuanaco and Huari c.500.

Huari abandoned c.800.

Decline of Tiahuanaco c.1000.

Carib Indians arrive in Antilles c.1200.

Inca city of Cuzco founded 1200.

Columbus lands in Bahamas 1492.

Spaniards conquer Peru and destroy Inca empire 1532.

ANCIENT AMERICA

From the Arctic Ocean in the north of the Americas to the extreme tip of South America is a distance of about 9,000 miles (14,500 km). Across this huge distance there are noticeable differences in both climate and landscape. They change from vast frozen plains to fertile river valleys, lush tropical forests, grasslands, and endless deserts. Mountains run along almost the whole length of the west coast of both North and South America.

The Native Americans, who arrived long before the European explorers, had to learn to be flexible and to adapt in order to survive in these very different environments.

Hunters and Farmers

Some of the early Native American peoples were nomadic hunters and gatherers, such as the Shoshone. They lived in the deserts west of the Rocky Mountains and moved around to find animals and plants to eat. They carried their few possessions with them and camped in simple shelters made from brushwood.

Other early peoples, such as the Aztec, settled in permanent villages in the fertile Valley of Mexico. They lived close to their fields, which they cultivated to grow most of their food. They were ferocious warriors, who, within a relatively short time period, defeated their neighbors and seized their lands to increase the size of their own empire. At its peak, the vast Aztec Empire spread across much of Central America and dominated the region for about 100 years.

RIGHT: The Rocky Mountains and the Andes are part of the mountain chain that runs down the western side of the American continents like a giant backbone. The mountains on the eastern side are less dramatic, with the Appalachian Mountains in the north and the Brazilian Highlands in the south. In between, the land is mainly low-lying with broad valleys drained by great rivers, such as the Mississippi, the Amazon, and the Orinoco.

BELOW: The rain forests of Ecuador are lush and fertile. The original peoples who lived there were hunters and farmers who cut down trees and burned the undergrowth to make clearings where they could plant crops and build houses. When the land was used up or exhausted, they simply moved on to clear another part of the forest.

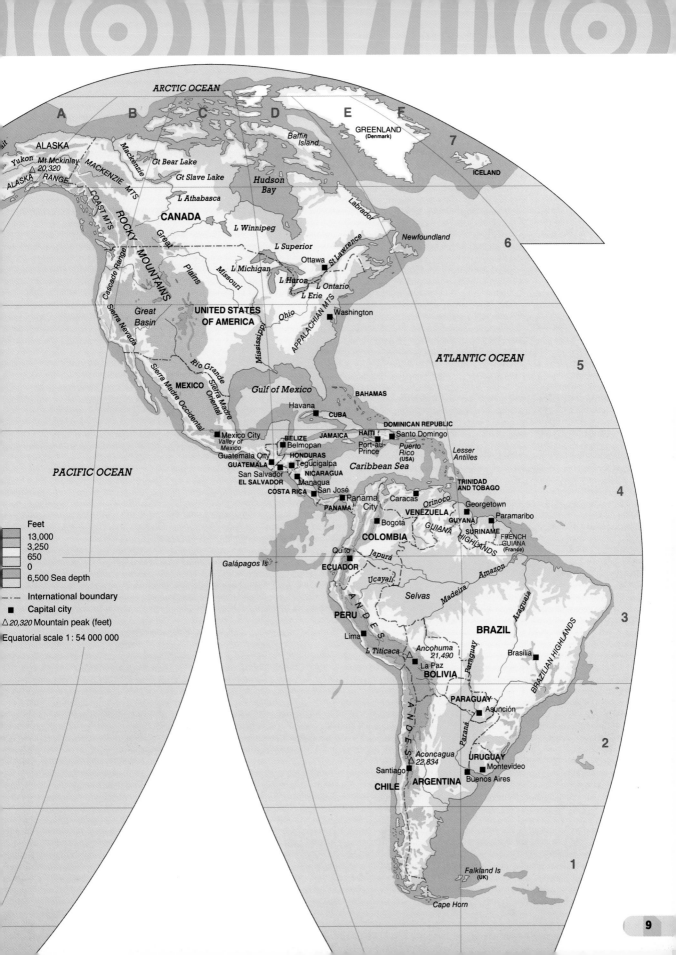

ARCTIC OCEAN

A   B   C   D   E   F

GREENLAND
(Denmark)

7

Baffin Island

ALASKA

Yukon Mt Mckinley
△ 20,320
ALASKA RANGE

MACKENZIE MTS

Mackenzie

Gt Bear Lake

Gt Slave Lake

Hudson Bay

ICELAND

COAST MTS

ROCKY MOUNTAINS

Great

Cascade Range

Sierra Nevada

CANADA

L Athabasca

L Winnipeg

L Superior

L Michigan

Missouri

Plains

Ottawa

St Lawrence

Labrador

Newfoundland

6

UNITED STATES
OF AMERICA

L Huron

L Ontario

L Erie

Ohio

Washington

APPALACHIAN MTS

Great Basin

Mississippi

Gulf of Mexico

ATLANTIC OCEAN

5

Rio Grande

Sierra Madre Oriental

MEXICO

Sierra Madre Occidental

BAHAMAS

Havana

CUBA

DOMINICAN REPUBLIC

Mexico City
Valley of Mexico

BELIZE

JAMAICA

HAITI

Santo Domingo

Belmopan

Port-au-Prince

Puerto Rico (USA)

Lesser Antilles

Guatemala City

HONDURAS

PACIFIC OCEAN

GUATEMALA

Tegucigalpa

Caribbean Sea

San Salvador

NICARAGUA

EL SALVADOR

Managua

TRINIDAD AND TOBAGO

COSTA RICA

San José

Panama City

Caracas

Georgetown

4

PANAMA

Orinoco

Paramaribo

VENEZUELA

GUYANA

Bogotá

GUIANA HIGHLANDS

SURINAME

FRENCH GUIANA
(France)

COLOMBIA

Quito

Japurá

ECUADOR

Amazon

Galápagos Is

Ucayali

Selvas

Madeira

Araguaia

BRAZIL

BRAZILIAN HIGHLANDS

A N D E S

PERU

Lima

Paraguay

Brasília

3

L Titicaca

Ancohuma
21,490
△

La Paz

BOLIVIA

PARAGUAY

Asunción

Paraná

2

A N D E S

Aconcagua
△ 22,834

URUGUAY

Santiago

Montevideo

CHILE

ARGENTINA

Buenos Aires

Falkland Is (UK)

1

Cape Horn

Feet
13,000
3,250
650
0
6,500 Sea depth

— ·· — International boundary
■ Capital city
△20,320 Mountain peak (feet)
Equatorial scale 1 : 54 000 000

FIRST AMERICANS

We still are not really sure how and when the first people arrived in the Americas. Our knowledge depends on finding ancient remains, but archaeological discoveries from ancient sites are rare. From the ancient remains that have been discovered, such as the stone tools found at Meadowcroft Rock Shelter in Pennsylvania, and the remains of an early campsite uncovered at Monte Verde in Chile, archaeologists have dated the presence of early humans as far back as 16,000 years ago.

Waves of Migrants

During the last Ice Age, Asia and the Americas were not separated by sea as they are now. They were linked by a land bridge that was around 900 miles (1,440 km) wide, known to scientists as Beringia. Early man crossed Beringia from Asia to America on foot, probably in pursuit of large herds of Ice Age grazing animals, such as the mammoth, mastodon, caribou, and bison, which also crossed over the grassland bridge.

It was these small bands of nomadic hunters, the ancestors of the Native Americans, that were likely the first arrivals in the Americas.

Archaeologists think that the migrants came in small groups over a long period of time. This theory is backed up by genetic and linguistic data, some of which suggests that people may, in fact, have lived in the Americas for an even longer period than the archaeological evidence indicates. Some of the early people may have arrived by boat along the Pacific coast of Alaska and Canada. However, it is highly unlikely that people traveled across the North Atlantic.

During the last Ice Age, so much water turned to ice that sea level fell, exposing dry land in many places. Where the Bering Strait now divides Asia and America, there was a broad grassy plain known as Beringia, enabling people and animals to cross. To the south of Beringia, the way was blocked by ice. Some archaeologists believe that in about 10,000 BCE some of the ice melted, opening up a new corridor along which people moved southward into the Americas. However, sites such as Meadowcroft and Monte Verde suggest that people had already moved south some 6,000 years earlier.

ASIA

Pack ice

BERINGIA

CORDILLERAN ICE SHEET

LAURENTIDE ICE SHEET

Retreat of ice sheets during last Ice Age

——— 18,000–16,000 B.C.E.

-------- 10,000 B.C.E.

·········· 6000 B.C.E

➤ Possible ice-free route south taken by first Americans, c.10,000 B.C.E.

After the Ice Age

When the last Ice Age ended, ice sheets melted and sea levels rose across the planet. Beringia, the land bridge that separated Asia from the Americas, was submerged in about 10,000 BCE, and the first campsites of the migrants were lost under the rising waters. People who arrived in America after this time, such as the Inuit, could no longer walk across the land bridge and had to cross from Asia by boat.

By then, other groups of hunters had spread to the far south. Archaeologists have discovered traces of their temporary campsites, which include chipped stone points perhaps used for

The first people to inhabit the cold plains of Ice Age America were small bands of nomadic hunters. The animals they hunted with their stone-tipped spears provided food for their families, as well as skins for making tents and warm clothing.

hunting, at the New Mexico sites of Clovis and Folsom, and also at the South Carolina site of Topper. By 10,000 BCE, people had traveled as far south as the tip of South America.

When the climate changed, forests began to replace grasslands in many regions, and large animals, such as the mammoth, died out because they no longer had vast pastures on which to graze.

NORTH AMERICA AFTER THE ICE AGE

With the change in climate, big game animals, such as the horse, the mammoth, and the mastodon, had died out by 8000 BCE. For food, people started to hunt a larger range of smaller animals. As they no longer needed to follow the big game herds for their food, their lives became more settled and less nomadic.

Early man also started to hunt for food in particular areas and to make the most of the different sources of food found throughout the year. At this stage, they did not know how to grow their own crops. Instead, they collected wild plants to eat. This period of development is known as the Archaic Period.

Hunting and Fishing

Caribou and deer were the most important animals for Archaic hunters. As well as providing meat, the animal skins were used for clothing and other useful items. Early man also hunted smaller game such as rabbits, otters, beavers, raccoons, and several types of birds. For those who lived near water, the sea, lakes, and rivers supplied all kinds of fish and shellfish.

As people took on these different activities, they began to make more specialized weapons and tools to use. The hunter's favorite tool was a stone-tipped spear. Sometimes, a spear-thrower would be used (see page 14). This was a device that allowed the spear to be thrown further and harder than if it was thrown in the normal way. Hunters also made nets, traps, and snares, using them to catch small mammals, birds, and fish.

Using Plants

In addition to meat and fish, fruits, seeds, and nuts were an important food source for early man. Seeds and nuts were ground between stones to make coarse flour, which may have been used to make bread or porridge. From about 2500 BCE, people in the North American Midwest also began to cultivate plants, such as squashes, sunflowers, and goosefoot. People ate the plants to supplement the meat that they hunted, the fish that they caught, and the wild foods that they gathered.

People wove baskets, mats, and bags from grass and reeds. They coated some baskets with clay to make them waterproof. They may have used the baskets to cook their food by filling the baskets with water and then heating the water. They did this by dropping hot stones or balls of clay inside, which then heated up the water. This type of cooking was called 'stone boiling', and it continued in some regions of North America up until 100 years ago. In the eastern part of the present-day United States, pottery came into use around 2500 BCE.

Following the Seasons

People still moved according to the seasons. They had special places they returned to every

Ancient Native American hunter-gatherers prepare and cook food. As well as hunting for game animals and fish, seeds and nuts would be ground down between stones to make flour, which, in turn, would be used to make bread or porridge. The illustration shows some of the tools that were used, as well as a basket woven from reeds, which was used for collecting wild plants.

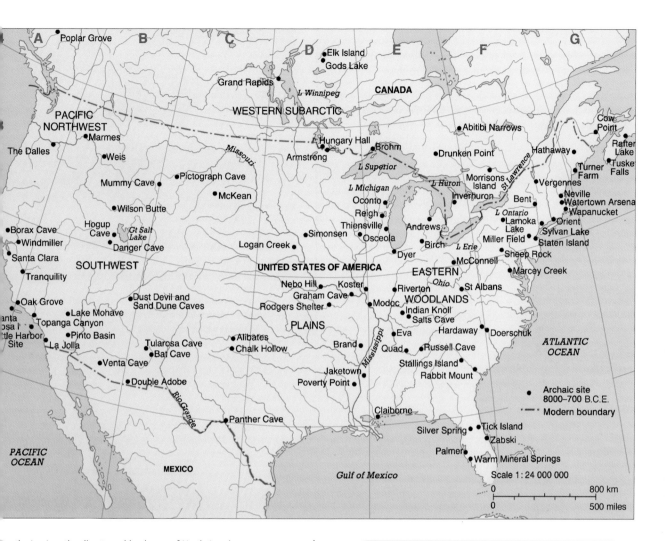

A Poplar Grove
B
C
D Elk Island
Gods Lake
Grand Rapids
L Winnipeg
CANADA
E
F
G
Cow Point
PACIFIC NORTHWEST
WESTERN SUBARCTIC
Abitibi Narrows
Rafter Lake
Marmes
Hungary Hall
Brohm
Drunken Point
Hathaway
Turner Farm
Tuske Falls
The Dalles
Missouri
Armstrong
L Superior
Morrisons Island
St Lawrence
Vergennes
Weis
Mummy Cave
Pictograph Cave
L Huron
L Michigan
Inverhuron
Bent
Neville
Watertown Arsena
McKean
Oconto
L Ontario
Wapanucket
Wilson Butte
Reigh
Lamoka Lake
Orient
Hogup Cave
Gt Salt Lake
Thiensville
Andrews
Miller Field
Sylvan Lake
Borax Cave
Simonsen
Osceola
Staten Island
Windmiller
Danger Cave
Logan Creek
Birch
L Erie
Sheep Rock
Santa Clara
Dyer
McConnell
Marcey Creek
Tranquility
SOUTHWEST
UNITED STATES OF AMERICA
EASTERN
Ohio
St Albans
Nebo Hill
Koster
Riverton
Oak Grove
Graham Cave
WOODLANDS
anta
Dust Devil and Sand Dune Caves
Rodgers Shelter
Modoc
Indian Knoll
osa l
Lake Mohave
Salts Cave
ttle Harbor
Topanga Canyon
PLAINS
Eva
Hardaway
Doerschuk
Site
Pinto Basin
Alibates
Brand
Russell Cave
ATLANTIC OCEAN
La Jolla
Tularosa Cave
Chalk Hollow
Quad
Venta Cave
Bat Cave
Jaketown
Stallings Island
Double Adobe
Poverty Point
Rabbit Mount
Rio Grande
Mississippi
Claiborne
Archaic site 8000–700 B.C.E.
Panther Cave
Modern boundary
Silver Spring
Tick Island
PACIFIC OCEAN
Zabski
Palmer
MEXICO
Gulf of Mexico
Warm Mineral Springs
Scale 1 : 24 000 000
0   800 km
0   500 miles

ter the Ice Age, the climate and landscape of North America
came similar to those of today. People began to follow new ways
life. Some remained nomadic, constantly on the move in search
food, but in areas where there were plenty of animals and plants
eat, many people chose to remain in one place at least for part
the year. This map shows some of the places where they settled.

ar. In the Eastern Woodlands, people settled
 permanent base camps or villages during the
inter and then returned to them after long
unting trips during the summer months.

    People who lived in the deserts of the North
merican Southwest would move from one cave
elter to another throughout the year. Often
ey left heavy tools and food supplies in each
ive so they did not have to carry everything
ith them as they traveled. Some of these
ored items have survived for 10,000 years.

Life in the Archaic Period 8000–1000 BCE

Subarctic - Hunting, fishing, and gathering people, who lived in small campsites.

Eastern Woodlands - Hunting and gathering people, who lived in winter villages, and traveled to summer campsites.

Plains - Nomadic buffalo hunters, who lived in small, temporary campsites, and followed buffalo herds.

Northwest Coast - Hunting and fishing people, who lived in winter villages, and traveled to summer campsites.

Southwestern Deserts - Hunting and gathering people, who also fished along the western coastlines of North America. They made use of cave shelters and campsites.

THE ARCTIC

The last native people who moved into North America from Asia around 4000 BCE were ancestors of today's Inuit people. From present-day Alaska, they traveled eastward along the central Arctic coast and reached Greenland by about 2500 BCE. Most of the modern Inuit people are probably distantly related to these early people.

The early Inuit people lived as nomadic hunters and fishermen. In some of their campsites, archaeologists have found small, delicately worked tools and weapons, and the bones of the animals that they hunted.

The Eastern Arctic

A group of people, named the Dorset people, spread across much of Canada and Greenland from about 1000 BCE. They take their name from Cape Dorset on Baffin Island. The Dorset people hunted seals, walrus, and caribou. During the

The Inuit used several kinds of harpoons and spears. A walrus harpoon had to be very strong to pierce the animal's thick hide. Spears used for hunting seals and birds were smaller and lighter. Hunters also invented wooden spear-throwers (above) to increase the spear's power and range. Each one was specially made for the hunter using it—its length equaled the distance between his forefinger and his elbow, and, in effect, gave him an extra arm jo

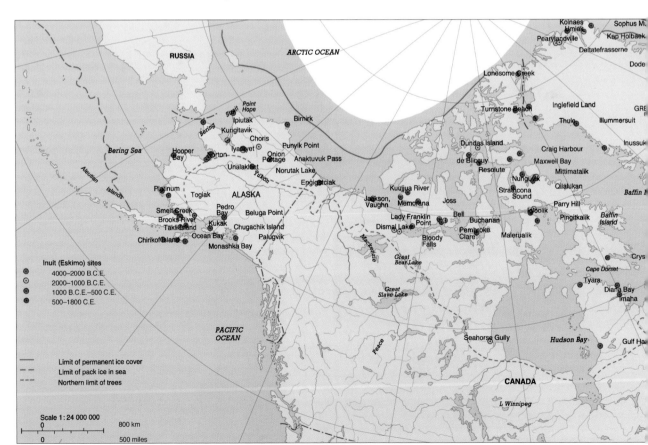

Inuit (Eskimo) sites
- 4000–2000 B.C.E.
- 2000–1000 B.C.E.
- 1000 B.C.E.–500 C.E.
- 500–1800 C.E.

— Limit of permanent ice cover
– – Limit of pack ice in sea
--- Northern limit of trees

Scale 1 : 24 000 000
0   800 km
0   500 miles

ummer, they went on long hunting trips and
ved in tents made from animal skins. They
vented sleds, but, since they did not have any
ogs to pull them, they had to pull the sleds
nemselves. During the freezing winter months,
ne Dorset people lived in villages. Their houses
ere built partly underground for warmth, and
ne walls were constructed from turf covered with
nimal skins. Inside each house, in the middle of
ne floor, there was an open hearth or fireplace.
round the inner walls of the house were benches
r people to sit or sleep on.

ne Western Arctic

om around 500 BCE, large villages were built
ong the Alaskan coast. Ipiutak, located on
pint Hope, may have had as many as 700
buses. In the burial ground in Ipiutak, many
eautiful walrus bone and ivory carvings have
een found. The Alaskan (Okvik) people used

kayaks, or light canoes, which they constructed
by stretching animal skins tightly over a wooden
framework. These craft were used to hunt seal
and walrus. They also hunted whales, but in
much larger open boats called umiaks. The
Dorset people used dogs to pull their sleds,
and were also skilled carvers in ivory.

The Romans gave the far north the name
Thule, which is also the name given to late
prehistoric Arctic peoples. The Thule people of
Alaska were very clever hunters who invented
new types of harpoons and boats for hunting
sea mammals, especially whales.

Around 1000 CE, the Thule people started
to move eastward. They may have taken land
by force and conquered the inhabitants. This
theory comes from Inuit legends that tell stories
about an earlier race of giants, the Tunit, who
were driven away after brutal battles with Inuit
ancestors. The stories may refer to encounters
between the Dorset and Thule peoples.

Most Inuit have always lived along the coasts of the tundra region, the treeless land beyond the northern limits of forest. The animals they hunted supplied them with all their needs. Over several thousands of years, the Inuit perfected a way of life that is ideally suited to the harsh Arctic environment.

Settlement in the Arctic
4000 BCE–1500 CE

c.4000–3000 BCE – The first Inuit begin to move into North America from Asia.

c.2000 BCE – Inuit people reach northernmost Greenland.

c.1000 BCE–1000 CE – The Dorset people spread out over the eastern Arctic.

c.500 BCE–500 CE – Large villages, such as Ipiutak, are built along the coast of western Alaska.

c.100 BCE–100 CE – Okvik people settle in northern Alaska.

c.500–1000 CE – The Thule people arrive in Alaska and spread all across the northern Arctic to Greenland.

c.985 CE – Norse settlers arrive in Greenland.

c.1000–1500 CE – The Thule people spread across the Arctic from Alaska to Greenland.

c.1400 CE – Norse settlements in Greenland are abandoned.

THE BURIAL MOUND BUILDERS

By 1000 BCE, there were many well-organized farming settlements in the Eastern Woodlands region of North America. The inhabitants grew their own crops, as well as continuing to gather wild plants. The Adena lived in the Ohio Valley from about 700 BCE. They hunted, fished, and grew a variety of food crops, such as squash and gourds. The Hopewell, who followed in around 100 BCE, also grew corn. Their culture extended as far as the Mississippi River and its tributaries.

Earthworks and Burial Mounds

The Adena and Hopewell farmers lived a settled life. The Hopewell built huge earthworks that still stand. Some were enclosures, perhaps built to hold important ceremonies. Others were most likely burial mounds. They contained log tombs, in which the dead were placed along with a variety of beautiful grave objects, such as necklaces, bracelets, and ear ornaments. The jewelry was made from precious metals such as

BELOW: The mounds at Etowah, Georgia, were constructed by Mississippian builders some 1,000 years after the Adena and Hopewell, showing how long the tradition of mound building lasted.

gold, silver, and copper, as well as pearls and shells. Also in the graves were stone tobacco pipes, and tools crafted from stone and copper. There were strange shapes cut from sheets of copper and mica, but their purpose is unclear.

Trading Networks

The quality of the objects found in the burial mounds shows that skilled craftsmen made them from rare and precious materials. Many of these materials came from a long way away. They were brought to the villages by a network of trade routes that stretched for hundreds of miles along rivers and tracks. These trails ran all the way from the Great Lakes in the north down to the Gulf of Mexico in the south, and west to the Rocky Mountains.

RIGHT: The Adena and Hopewell set up trading links with dist[ant] people to obtain raw materials, such as mica, copper, and she[ll]. Traders exchanged finished goods for raw materials. The peo[ple] who acquired these goods began to copy them and to follow [the] customs of their makers. This was how the way of life of the Ade[na] and Hopewell spread far beyond the Ohio Val[ley].

Trading Links Across North America

The raw materials used by the Adena and Hopewell peoples came from far-flung communities:

Stone came from various different areas. It was used for making tools, weapons, and tobacco pipes.

Copper and Silver came from the Great Lakes, and were used for making jewelry and musical instruments.

Mica came from the Appalachian Mountains. It was used for making cut-outs, shaped like hands, claws, and snakes.

Obsidian came from the Rocky Mountains. It is a glasslike rock used for making knives and spearheads.

Shells and Alligator Teeth came from the Gulf of Mexico region and were used to make necklaces.

Pottery came from south of the Appalachian Mountains.

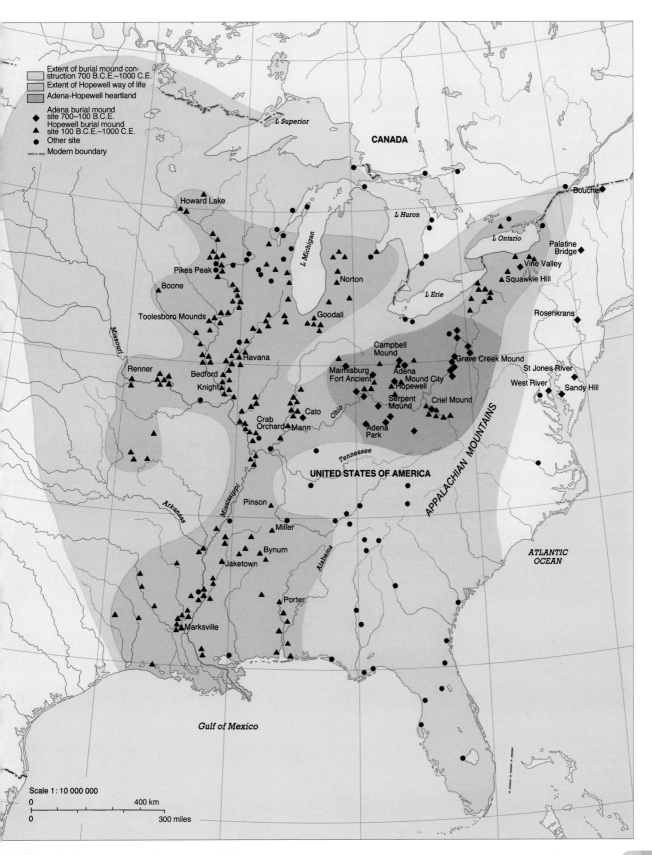

Extent of burial mound con-
struction 700 B.C.E.–1000 C.E.
Extent of Hopewell way of life
Adena-Hopewell heartland

◆ Adena burial mound
site 700–100 B.C.E.
▲ Hopewell burial mound
site 100 B.C.E.–1000 C.E.
● Other site
- - - Modern boundary

CANADA

L Superior

L Huron

L Michigan

L Ontario

L Erie

Howard Lake

Boucher

Palatine
Bridge

Vine Valley

Squawkie Hill

Norton

Pikes Peak

Boone

Rosenkrans

Toolesboro Mounds

Goodall

Campbell
Mound

Grave Creek Mound

St Jones River

Renner

Havana

Maimisburg
Fort Ancient

Adena

Mound City

West River

Sandy Hill

Bedford

Hopewell

Knight

Serpent
Mound

Criel Mound

Crab
Orchard

Cato

Mann

Adena
Park

Ohio

APPALACHIAN MOUNTAINS

Tennessee

UNITED STATES OF AMERICA

Arkansas

Mississippi

Pinson

ATLANTIC
OCEAN

Miller

Bynum

Alabama

Jaketown

Porter

Marksville

Gulf of Mexico

Scale 1 : 10 000 000

0   400 km

0   300 miles

17

TEMPLE MOUND BUILDERS

Around 1,400 years ago the farmers of the Eastern Woodlands started to grow a new type of corn. It came from Mexico and was stronger and produced better crops than the local corn. In some well-protected areas it could be planted and harvested twice in the same season. With this and other improvements in farming, the daily life of the communities became better. This era is known as the Mississippian Period.

Mississippian settlements were larger than those built by northern Native Americans and are now considered to be the first real towns in North America, because the settlements had thousands of inhabitants. A typical town usually consisted of a number of rectangular, flat-topped mounds, grouped around a plaza or square. The mounds were built from earth, with a ramp or stairway of logs that led to the top. Temples and houses were built on the top.

The Southern Cult

Many interesting objects have been found in the temple mounds of the southern Mississippi area, including disks made from shell, and copper sheets engraved with unusual designs. These designs include crosses, suns, weeping eyes, and hands with an eye in the center of the palm. It is thought that these were probably symbols of the Southern Cult, a mysterious religion about which little is known.

Temple Mound Sites 800–1500 CE

Villages These were usually built near to rivers and protected by palisades. Villages were concentrated around a central plaza surrounded by earth mounds, on top of which were constructed wooden temples and the houses of the village chiefs. Ordinary houses were built from wattle and daub and topped with thatched roofs.

Livelihood Most people in village communities farmed, but they also fished, hunted, and gathered wild plants.

Tools and Weapons These included digging sticks and hoes made of stone, bone, or shells, fastened to wooden handles. Bows and arrows were used for hunting. Lines with bone hooks and nets were used for fishing.

Costume People wore moccasins on their feet. Moccasins were made from animal skins or woven. Clothes were breechcloth (like a loincloth), or a skirt and a cloak. Jewelry was popular, and people wore ear ornaments, necklaces, and bracelets made from stone, bone, shells, and copper.

RIGHT: The way of life of the Mississippian people was based on the intensive farming of corn. It was no accident that a number of Mississippian colonies spread out from the Middle Mississippi along the fertile river valleys where corn could be grown. Temple mounds similar to those in the Middle Mississippi area are also found in these outlying regions.

BELOW: Important people were often buried under the floors of the temples that were built on the flat-topped mounds. Others, as here, were buried in cemeteries near the towns. Grave goods—pottery, shell, or copper ornaments—were placed around the bodies.

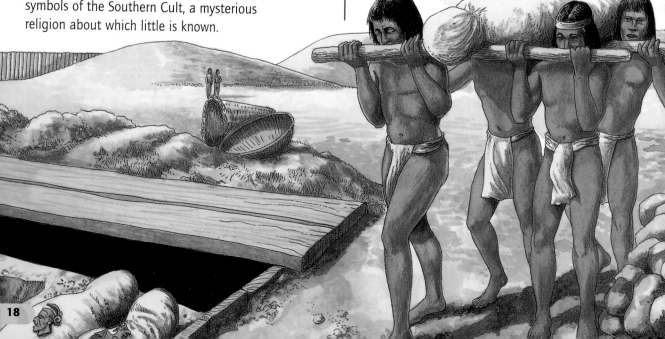

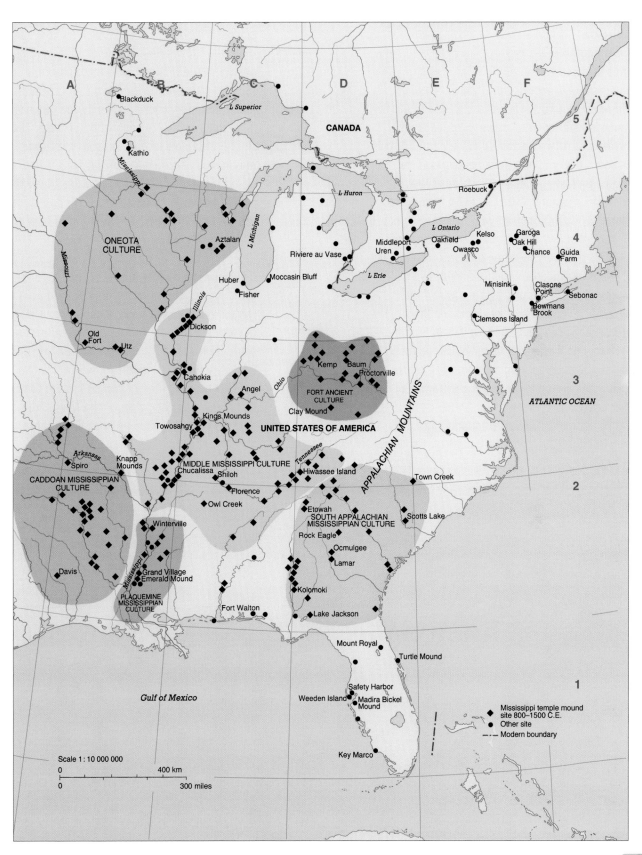

ONEOTA CULTURE

CANADA

L Superior

Blackduck

Kathio

Mississippi

Missouri

L Michigan

L Huron

Roebuck

L Ontario

Middleport
Uren

Oakfield
Owasco

Kelso

Garoga
Oak Hill
Chance

Guida
Farm

Riviere au Vase

Aztalan

Huber
Fisher

Moccasin Bluff

L Erie

Minisink

Clasons
Point

Sebonac

Bowmans
Brook

Clemsons Island

Old
Fort

Utz

Illinois

Dickson

Cahokia

Angel

Ohio

Kemp   Baum
        Proctorville

FORT ANCIENT
CULTURE

Clay Mound

Kings Mounds

Towosahgy

UNITED STATES OF AMERICA

Arkansas

Spiro

CADDOAN MISSISSIPPIAN
CULTURE

Knapp
Mounds

MIDDLE MISSISSIPPI CULTURE
Chucalissa   Shiloh

Florence

Owl Creek

Tennessee

Hiwassee Island

Town Creek

APPALACHIAN MOUNTAINS

ATLANTIC OCEAN

Davis

Winterville

Mississippi

Grand Village
Emerald Mound

PLAQUEMINE
MISSISSIPPIAN
CULTURE

Fort Walton

Etowah
SOUTH APPALACHIAN
MISSISSIPPIAN CULTURE

Rock Eagle

Ocmulgee

Lamar

Kolomoki

Lake Jackson

Scotts Lake

Mount Royal

Turtle Mound

Gulf of Mexico

Safety Harbor

Weeden Island   Madira Bickel
                 Mound

Key Marco

◆ Mississippi temple mound
   site 800–1500 C.E.
● Other site
–·– Modern boundary

Scale 1: 10 000 000

0   400 km

0   300 miles

Mound Sites

Cahokia

Near to the modern city of St Louis, in the present-day state of Missouri, are the remains a large Native American settlement, known as Cahokia. It was founded in about 600 CE, and in its heyday was the largest prehistoric city north of Mexico. At its peak, in around 1100 CE, there were as many as 10,000 people living there.

Cahokia has more than 100 human-made mounds that vary in shape and size. The largest of these earthworks, which is known as Monk's Mound, is a flat-topped pyramid with four terraces. It rises up to a height of 100 feet (30 m) above the surrounding valley. Building the mounds was labor-intensive. The builders had no carts or pack animals to assist them. Instead, they had to transport the earth for the mounds in baskets.

In about 1200 CE, a wooden fence was constructed around the central plaza. The fence enclosed Monk's Mound, as well as 16 smaller mounds. The wooden buildings that were built on top of the mounds were most probably temples, or were the houses of important people within Cahokia. Some of the mounds have been shown to contain burial sites. The smaller mounds, located outside the fence, may have been the sites of the houses and burial mounds of less important people within the community. Pits that had been dug during the construction of the mounds were later used to store water.

Government and Trade

Cahokia was the most significant town in the region and was also probably the seat of government for the surrounding area until the settlement started to decline around 1450 CE. In addition to this important administrative center, there were a number of smaller towns situated along the banks of the Mississippi and along the other rivers that flowed into it near Cahokia.

Small hamlets of wattle and daub houses (right) were scattered over the fertile river plain around Cahokia. These were the homes of the farmers who supplied the city with food. In their fields, the farmers grew corn, beans, and squash—a kind of marrow. The farmers stored their surplus crops in pits dug into the ground outside their houses.

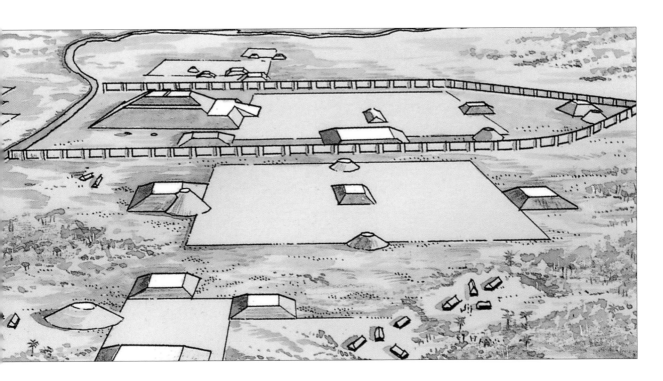

Cahokia was also an important trading center, as grave goods that have been found in some of the burial mounds testify. These include copper items from the Great Lakes, mica from the Appalachian Mountains, and shells from the East Coast.

Emerald Mound

Emerald Mound was one of at least nine towns that were once inhabited by the Natchez Indians. It lies in the Lower Mississippi valley, near to the present-day city of Natchez. We know more about the Natchez Indians than other Native American communities because French explorers visited the Natchez in the early 18th century. They wrote about what they saw and how the Natchez lived. Only a few years after they visited, the Natchez were almost completely destroyed by disease and warfare.

The Natchez Indians may have been the descendants of the earlier Mound Builders.

Emerald Mound is a natural hill that was flattened to make a large platform 770 feet (230 m) long and 440 feet (130 m) wide. Two flat-topped earthen pyramids were built on the top. The larger of these two pyramids is almost 33 feet (10 m) tall.

Cahokia consists of more than 100 mounds. Monk's Mound is one of the largest human-made earthworks in North America. It contains about 780,000 cubic yards (600,000 cu. m) of earth, and at its base measures 990 x 660 feet (300 x 200 m)—more than 12 times the area of a modern soccer field.

They were ruled by a powerful chief who was known as the Great Sun. He wore an elaborate feather headdress and a magnificent cloak, also made from beautiful feathers. He did not walk anywhere, but was carried in a litter by his subjects, who treated him with great reverence. Anyone who made him angry was put to death. When the Great Sun died, his wife and servants were killed and buried with him.

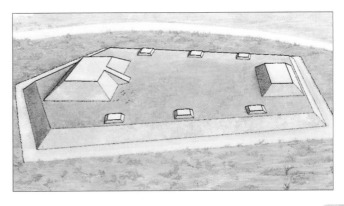

THE NORTHERN IROQUOIANS

The Northern Iroquoians lived in woodlands to the northeast of the Mississippian people. By about 1000 CE, the Iroquoians had spread over a large area around the eastern Great Lakes and along the St Lawrence river valley. When the earliest European explorers first encountered the Iroquoians in the 16th century, the Native American people had divided themselves into 12 separate tribes.

Village Life

The Iroquoians lived in villages and hunted in the local woods for deer, bear, and caribou. They also trapped smaller animals like rabbits and beavers, and traded goods with other Native Americans. The women worked in the fields, using hoes and digging sticks to prepare and cultivate the soil before planting the seeds. There were three main food crops, known as the "three sisters"—corns, beans, and squash. The fields were planted with crops for between 10 and 15 years, after which the soil was no longer fertile and the fields had to be abandoned. The men then cleared another part of the forest to create new fields and built a new village close by.

Early Iroquoian villages were built on the banks of streams or rivers. Later, to protect from possible attack by neighboring tribes, they built their villages on hilltops and surrounded them with wooden palisades, arranged in three rows with watchtowers between them. We know this from an account written by a 17th-century missionary, Gabriel Sagard, who lived and worked among the Huron people.

Sometimes, villages joined together for trade, or to fight against a common enemy, but there was no central government within a tribe. An elected chief ruled each village with a council to advise him and help to keep order.

Longhouses

An Iroquoian village consisted of a number of longhouses. Several related families all lived together in one longhouse. The longhouses were built using frameworks of wooden poles covered by sheets of tree bark. The buildings were of different sizes, but a house for 20 families might be as long as 150 feet (46 m).

The inside of the longhouse was divided up so that each family could have its own section measuring 13 feet (4 m) long, and divided by a partition from its neighbors. Food and firewood were stored at one end of the house. In the center of the house there were racks where families could keep their belongings—clothes, hunting weapons, farming tools, baskets,

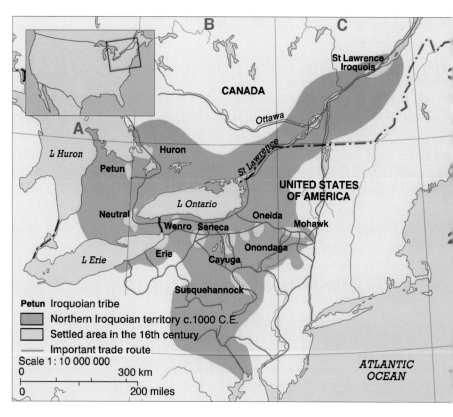

The 12 tribes of Northern Iroquoians lived around the eastern Great Lakes and along the St Lawrence valley.

Petun Iroquoian tribe
Northern Iroquoian territory c.1000 C.E.
Settled area in the 16th century
Important trade route
Scale 1 : 10 000 000
0   300 km
0   200 miles

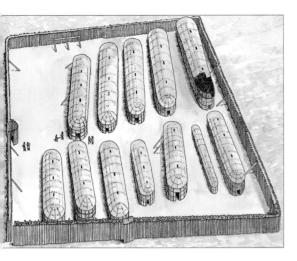

...e Mohawk village of Caughnawaga, built about 1690 CE. Earlier ...lages were larger, with perhaps 50 longhouses occupied by as ...ny as 2,000 people. This site, west of the Hudson River, is a ...e, completely preserved Iroquois village.

...ooking pots, utensils, and birchback bowls for ...erving food. Low wooden benches covered with ...kins lined the walls. These were for sitting ...n and for sleeping. In the winter people slept ...nder their benches to keep warm. Two families ...hared a fireplace. The fireplaces were placed ...long the middle of the longhouse. Gaps in ...e roof allowed the smoke to escape.

...he Fur Trade

...he Iroquoian people were fur traders, while the ...uron traded corn, tobacco, and fishing nets in ...xchange for meat and fur. The Iroquoians had ...o travel long distances by river and on foot to ...unt for furs and then to trade them.

Following the arrival of French and English ...aders in the Eastern Woodlands in the 16th ...entury, the fur trade became very important, ...ecause fur was vital to keep people warm. The ...uropean traders traded goods such as beads, ...oth, metal tools, and guns in exchange for fur.

Iroquoian clothing was made from skins and furs. In warm weather, men, their bodies painted and tattooed, wore only a deerskin breechcloth and moccasins. In the winter months they wore a cloak, long sleeves, and leggings. This Iroquoian male carries a carved wooden club with a heavy rounded end.

As the fur trade rapidly grew, intense rivalry between the Iroquoian tribes for control of the precious trade routes eventually led to fighting between them. Many Iroquoians were killed in these battles, and many more died as a result of being exposed to European diseases, such as smallpox, to which Native Americans were being exposed for the first time. So many Iroquoians died that their populations shrank dramatically, and by the time French and English colonists arrived in the Woodlands area in the 17th century they found whole regions that were no longer inhabited.

During the 18th century, the Iroquoian federation of six tribes largely sided with the British in their wars against the French and later against the Americans.

THE GREAT PLAINS

The vast area that lies in the center of the North American continent is known as the Great Plains, and stretches all the way from the Mississippi River in the east to the Rocky Mountains in the west. From prehistoric times right up to the start of the 16th century, most of the Plains Indians who inhabited this region were farmers. Most lived in established villages on the eastern prairies, while the High Plains to the west were home to a smaller number of Native Americans who lived as nomadic buffalo hunters.

The Eastern Prairies

As early as 500 BCE, people started to settle in the upper Mississippi valley and on the eastern prairies. By 1000 CE, farming villages had been established high up on terraces or bluffs along the valley. While the people lived high up, they grew crops on the flood plain below. The most important crops were corn, beans, and squash. To supplement their food supply, the villagers probably left home once or twice a year to go on hunting trips. The discovery of buffalo bone at village sites shows that buffalo were hunted.

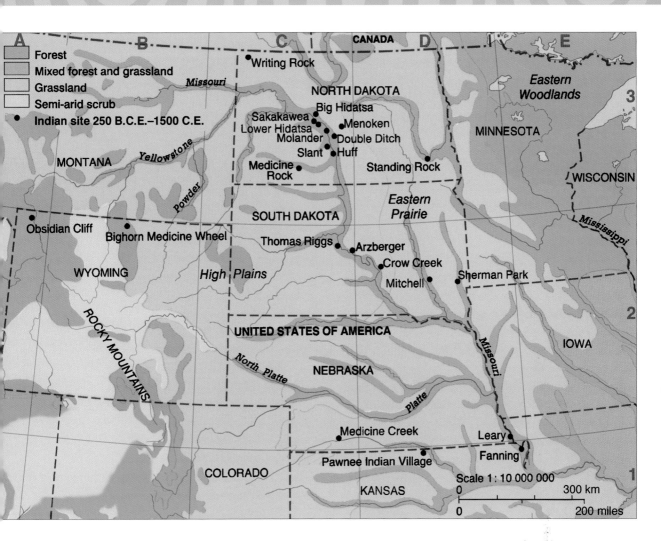

Forest
Mixed forest and grassland
Grassland
Semi-arid scrub
Indian site 250 B.C.E.–1500 C.E.

CANADA

Writing Rock

Missouri

NORTH DAKOTA

Big Hidatsa
Sakakawea
Lower Hidatsa · Menoken
Molander · Double Ditch
Slant · Huff
Medicine · Standing Rock
Rock

MONTANA

Yellowstone

Powder

MINNESOTA

Eastern Woodlands

WISCONSIN

Mississippi

Obsidian Cliff
Bighorn Medicine Wheel

SOUTH DAKOTA

Eastern Prairie

Thomas Riggs · Arzberger
· Crow Creek
Mitchell · Sherman Park

WYOMING

High Plains

UNITED STATES OF AMERICA

North Platte

NEBRASKA

Missouri

IOWA

ROCKY MOUNTAINS

Platte

Medicine Creek

Leary
Fanning

COLORADO

Pawnee Indian Village

KANSAS

Scale 1 : 10 000 000
0   300 km
0   200 miles

...uch bones were also used as tools. The main
...arming tool was a hoe made from the shoulder
...one of a buffalo tied to a wooden handle.

...he High Plains

...here was not enough rain to cultivate crops in
...he western Plains. Instead, the Native
...mericans were nomadic hunters. They followed
...he buffalo herds on foot and set up camp in
...kin tents. They did not have many possessions,

*...om the 15th century, Plains farmers lived in large dome-shaped
...rth lodges. Like their earlier houses, these were built from wood
...overed with turf and earth. Entry was through a covered passage.
...side, there was a central fireplace with a smoke hole in the roof
...bove. Raised wooden platforms running along the walls were
...ed as benches or beds. Before the reintroduction of the horse to
...e American continent, Prairie tribes used dogs for hunting, for
...ulling "travois" (sleds), and for carrying lightweight loads.*

*Before the Europeans arrived, most of the Plains Indians were
farmers. They grew corn and other crops along the river valleys
of the eastern Plains, where the soil was light and easily worked
with their farming tools, such as hoes and digging sticks. The
richer, heavier soil of the prairies was not cultivated until the
arrival of European plows and draft animals. In the western or
High Plains, there were only a few nomadic Native Americans,
who were hunters all the year around.*

because these had to be carried on their backs
or pulled by their dogs. The dogs were trained
to pull a type of sled known as a "travois."

When the 16th-century Spanish explorer
Francisco de Coronado arrived in the area, he
wrote scathingly of the Plains Indians whom he
met: "They do not plant anything and do not
have any houses except of skin and sticks and
they wander around with the cows."

THE FAR WEST

Between the Rocky Mountains and the Sierra Nevada, to the west of the Great Plains, is an immense wilderness made up mainly of desert and mountains. This difficult terrain meant that the Native Americans could not farm the land, as it was just too dry to support agriculture and, therefore, human settlements.

The Great Basin

The southern part of the Far West is known as the Great Basin. Only small groups of hunters and gatherers lived here, scattered across a vast area. Within these groups, both the men and women were responsible for getting food. The women foraged among the sparse vegetation for seeds and nuts, which they would grind into flour in order to to make porridge or bread.

The men hunted rabbits, birds, lizards, and even rats, as well as searching for insects such as grasshoppers and caterpillars. Large game, such as deer, was hard to find.

Since finding food was so difficult in this challenging landscape, people had to move constantly. During the summer months they lived along the banks of shallow lakes and streams, in shelters they constructed from brush. During the winter, when temperatures plunged, they camped in rock shelters or caves in the mountains. At each campsite, supplies of dried fruit and meat were kept in storage pits in readiness for their next visit.

The Plateau

To the north of the Great Basin, at the headwaters of the Columbia and Fraser Rivers, is a region of grassland and mountains known as the Plateau. The rivers were vital as a source of food for the Plateau Indians, as they teemed with fish, especially salmon. The Plateau Indians also hunted deer, antelope, and mountain sheep, and also gathered wild fruits and plants. The bulb of the camass lily (a close relative of the hyacinth) was one of their most important sources of food.

The variety of food available and the fact that it was easier to find than in other regions,

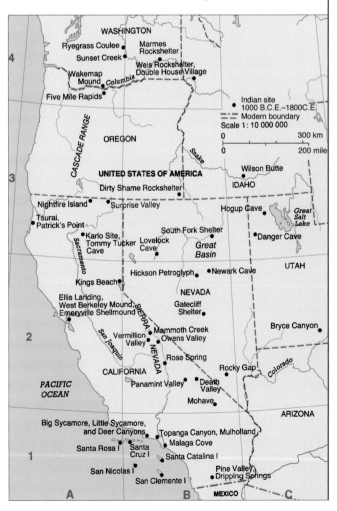

Prehistoric settlement sites in present-day California are located mainly on the coast and along rivers.

LIFE IN THE WEST—1000 BCE-1800 CE

In the desert basin the people gathered seeds and nuts (mainly pine nuts). To collect plant roots, they used digging sticks. They hunted deer using bows and arrows, and smaller game using nets and traps. Their clothes were made from animal skins and plant fibers. Their cloaks and blankets were made from twisted strips of rabbit fur.

On the plateau the rivers were full of fish (especially salmon), which were caught using spears, nets, traps, and weirs. Bows and arrows were used for hunting. The people made baskets for carrying, storing, and cooking food. Clothing was made from skins, furs, and plant fibers.

California (500-1800 CE) Seeds and nuts (especially acorns) were ground into flour. The people caught shellfish, and fished with spears and bone and shellfish hooks along the coast. Bows and arrows were used for hunting. Houses were circular in shape with domes and thatched roofs.

eant the Plateau Indians were able to settle
communities. For part of the year they lived
villages of "earth lodges." In the summer
ey moved to camps close to the rivers to fish.

alifornia

ne area that we now know as California, which
es to the west of the Sierra Nevada, was full of
atural resources, so gathering food was not a
roblem. The rivers and Pacific Ocean supplied
wide variety of different kinds of fish, which
ne Native Americans caught using hooks and
pears. They also found shellfish in the rocks
nd they went out to sea in canoes to hunt
r seals, dolphins, and porpoises.

There was plenty of game in the valleys
nd the oak trees that covered the hills were
den with acorns, which formed the basis
f the diet of the Californian Indians. They
ounded the acorns into a flour, which was
oiled using hot stones to make a porridge.

The rich flora not only meant that food
athering was easier, it also gave the women
ts of material from which to make mats and

Acorns, the main food of the Californian Indians, were poisonous if not treated carefully. They were first pounded into flour, which was put into a basket and rinsed to remove the harmful acids. The Californian Indians made shelters from brushwood, as shown here.

baskets. The baskets were used for numerous
tasks. Some were for collecting and storing
food, while others were so finely woven that
they could hold water without it leaking, even
without being waterproofed with pitch. These
were used for cooking. Special baskets were also
made to offer as gifts to other tribes or for use
in ceremonies. These baskets were often very
beautiful, often finished with brightly colored
feathers and hung with clamshell beads.

Shell beads and feathers were used to
make jewelry. For special ceremonies, the
Californian Indians would paint their bodies
with natural plant dyes and would decorate
themselves with ornate feather cloaks and
colorful headdresses. Everyday clothing was
much simpler. The men wore loincloths and the
women wore skirts. When the weather turned
colder during the winter months they wore
robes made from rabbit skins.

Southwest Sites

Mesa Verde

A distinctive feature of the southwestern landscape is the mesa. Mesas are steep-sided hills with flat tops. One of the most famous of all the mesas is Mesa Verde, a national park in Colorado that was once the home of the Anasazi peoples.

During the 12th century, the Anasazi people built terraced houses in the shelter of the mesa's overhanging cliffs, where they lived within large communities that numbered hundreds of people. The design of the houses suggests they were built to provide protection against attack from other tribes in the area, as none of the lower levels of the buildings have doors or windows. The Anasazi used ladders to enter their houses. The people were farmers, and remains of fields and irrigation terraces suggest they grew crops on the flat top of the mesa.

Early in the 14th century the Anasazi people abandoned most of the cliff dwellings at Mesa Verde. This was probably for a number of reasons that included lack of water, the failure of their crops, and the arrival of new groups who fought them. The Anasazi also fought within their own communities.

Cliff Palace

The Cliff Palace is the most famous, as well as the biggest, of all the many ruins in Mesa Verde National Park. Although it is called a palace, because of its many rooms—there are more than 400—and stone towers, in fact, it was not.

Some of its massive walls reach four stories high. The rooms are small and often strangely shaped, with low ceilings. Some rooms have a door and window, but others are only accessible

The ruins of the Cliff Palace in Mesa Verde, once home to hundreds of Anasazi farmers and their families. The round structures are "kivas" (underground meeting rooms), but are now roofless.

e remains of the Anasazi cliff dwelling known as the ʼhite House in Canyon de Chelly appear almost overwhelmed the massive rock walls behind them.

a the roof. The rooms had different functions. ome were used for living (with one family in ach room), while others were used for food reparation and for the storage of corn.

The large number of kivas (circular nderground rooms) at the site suggests that ae Cliff Palace may have been a religious enter for the whole region. Kivas were where nen performed religious ceremonies and held neetings. Archaeologists are not sure what the tone towers were used for. They may have been ortress homes or perhaps observatories to ollow the position of the sun to calculate the est times for planting and harvesting crops.

anyon de Chelly

he spectacular Canyon de Chelly is another ncient site of the Anasazi people. It is located n northeastern Arizona in an area of mountain

ranges that are cut through with sheer-sided canyons, which are often more than 650 feet (200 m) deep. In the 12th century, Anasazi farmers built tall cliff houses within the shelter of the massive canyon walls. To reach the top of the canyon they cut climbing holes for their hands and feet into the sheer face of the cliff.

The Anasazi chose this location because the canyon floor was the most fertile farming land in the area. Their houses were all built so that they could keep a watch on their crops. Most of the houses faced south toward the sun. In the winters the dwellings remained warm, and in the summer months they were cool, because the overhanging cliffs protected them from the fierce rays of the sun.

Most of the cliff dwellings were quite small and could house no more than 30 or 40 people each. They contained living quarters, as well as storage rooms and kivas. Along an 18-mile (30-km) stretch of the Canyon de Chelly there are about 150 cliff dwellings built from sandstone blocks cut from the canyon walls.

Chaco Canyon

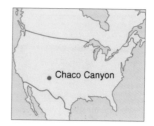

In an isolated part of northwestern New Mexico lies one of the greatest and most spectacular of all the Anasazi sites. Between 900 and 1100 CE, the Anasazi built 12 towns along Chaco Canyon, 95 miles (153 km) south of Mesa Verde. These towns were home to hundreds of people, who lived in multistory dwellings made from stone and adobe.

The towns were linked not only to each other by a series of roads, but also to the outside world so that the Anasazi could trade with other Native Americans. Goods, such as copper bells and brightly colored feathers, came from as far away as Mexico, and shells from the Pacific coast were also traded. Chaco Canyon also produced many valuable objects that were prized by other tribes. The towns were home to skilled craftsmen and women who worked as potters, weavers, basket makers, and carvers. They created beautiful cloaks out of feathers, and they carved shells, turquoise, and jet into a variety of decorative objects.

Pueblo Bonito

The largest and most spectacular of all the Chaco Canyon settlements is Pueblo Bonito. Early Spanish explorers named the town "pretty village" because they were so impressed by its appearance.

Pueblo Bonito was constructed facing south toward the Chaco River. It has a curving rear wall that was built against the cliff walls of the canyon. At its heart is a central plaza. Around the plaza are 800 rooms that were built in terraces. The roofs of the lower tiers provided open terraces for the upper stories.

The rooms rose to at least four stories above the ground level, with new rooms added later. The earliest rooms, at the back of the complex, became completely enclosed. As they had no windows, and the only way to get into them was through the roof, they were probably used for storage. Living rooms, in contrast, were larger and finished with plastered walls. Since few of the rooms had fireplaces, archaeologists think that cooking was probably done outdoors.

The large kivas (underground meeting rooms), some sunk into the central plaza, suggest that religious activity took place at Pueblo Bonito. Archaeologists have discovered many graves and ritual objects at the site.

Attack!

Although attack by other Native Americans was a constant threat, it is unclear which enemy the Anasazi feared. The Apache and Navajo, who raided the area in later centuries, did not yet live in the Southwest. However, to provide

Grass grows in the center of a ruined kiva at Chaco Canyon. The sunken kivas were ritual centers; they were usually entered by a ladder through a hole in the roof.

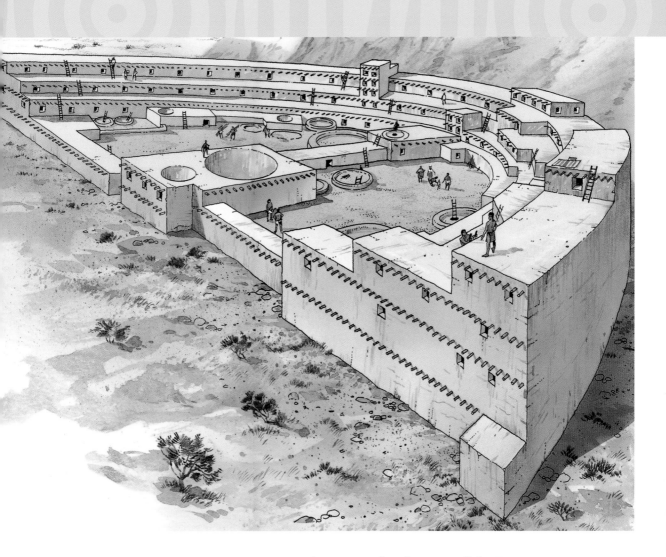

...eblo Bonito saw its heyday in the 12th century. The settlement ...n the shape of a huge "D", with its round back to the canyon ...ll. Entrance was by ladder. Archeologists now think that many ...er people lived here than was once believed. Instead of being ...stly residential, Pueblo Bonito may have served primarily as a ...cred site, a place of pilgrimage that drew visitors from a wide ...a. Its many kivas (underground meeting rooms) and evidence ...long-distance contacts support this interpretation.

...aximum protection, Pueblo Bonito was built ...ith defense firmly in mind. To this end, there ...ere no windows on the lowest level and none ...n the curved wall. Originally there was only ...he gateway. As time went on, this was made ...arrower and finally it was completely sealed. ...fter that, the only way to get into and ...ut of the town was by means of ladders. When ...ere was a threat of attack, the ladders could ...e pulled up by people from the inside.

Abandonment of the Towns

All Anasazi communities, including those in Chaco Canyon, were dependent on agriculture. Farmers collected rainwater, which was sent to the crop fields by a series of channels. When drought struck the Southwest during the last quarter of the 13th century, crops failed and daily life at Chaco Canyon started to collapse. By the early 14th century the Anasazi had left Chaco Canyon and moved to other areas.

Until the 19th century and the building of the first skyscrapers in Chicago and New York, Pueblo Bonito was the largest human-made housing structure in North America. Chaco Canyon was an important ceremonial and trade center, and archaeologists are still uncovering new information from the many outlying towns that have yet to be studied in detail.

NORTHWEST COAST

Between Southern Alaska and northern California, the Pacific Coast is made up of a narrow strip of land with many small islands, narrow beaches, and deep inlets. In many places, forests of spruce, cedar, and fir grow right up to the edge of the water. In other areas, high mountains loom over the shoreline.

Living off the Sea and Forests

The Native Americans who lived on the Northwest Coast were very lucky. The seas, rivers, and forests of the region provided them with almost all the food and shelter they needed. As well as fish and shellfish, they hunted whales, seals, sea lions, and porpoises. The forests provided the raw materials to make their homes, canoes, weapons, tools, boxes, and bowls. They even wove their clothing from strips of bark, as well as using it to make baskets and mats.

Ancient Settlements and Houses

Hunters and fishermen lived in this region 10,000 years ago. The Northwest Coast way of living emerged around 1000 BCE and lasted until the 19th century—almost 3,000 years. For most of the year the prehistoric Native Americans lived along the coastline just as their 19th century descendants (the Kwakiutl, Haida, Tsimshian, Tlingit, and others) would do. They mainly lived by fishing and hunting sea mammals, although they sometimes went inland to look for berries or to hunt deer and bears.

They lived in villages of large rectangular houses, which were built from wooden planks. Each house was home to a number of families who were all related, with a total of between 30 and 40 people in each dwelling. Every family had their own area within the house, which was separated from the other families by wooden screens or woven mats.

Totem Poles

An important industry for the Native American craftsmen was woodcarving. They used all kind of tools, such as hammers, adzes, chisels, awls, and drills. Originally their tools were made from stone, bone, and shell, before they obtained metal from traders and from European settlers. Unfortunately, not many of the early carvings survive, because wood rots easily in the damp climate of the Northwest. Only wood carved in the 19th century or later has survived.

The best known of all the woodcarvings are the totem poles. They were carved for different reasons. Some were a little like a medieval coat of arms, showing the emblems of a family, while others commemorated important events, or were a memorial to the dead. Some were used as posts around the front door of a house.

Masked Dancers and Potlatches

An important part of the ritual dances and ceremonies of the Native Americans were facemasks. Such masks are still used today. They were carved from wood and sometimes painted, and they often showed a supernatural being, in the form of an animal or bird that had come into contact with their ancestors. Many of the dances re-enacted family stories and legends about their ancestors. When the wearer put on a mask, he took on the personality of the spirit that he represented. In often very dramatic performances, the masked dancer might even swing through the air on ropes to give the illusion of flying.

Among many different types of masks, the most elaborate were known as "transformation masks. They were a kind of mask-within-a-mask. Often these masks were heavy and the wearer

An elaborately carved and painted Native American totem pole. Such totem poles were of great symbolic importance in the daily lives of Native American communities.

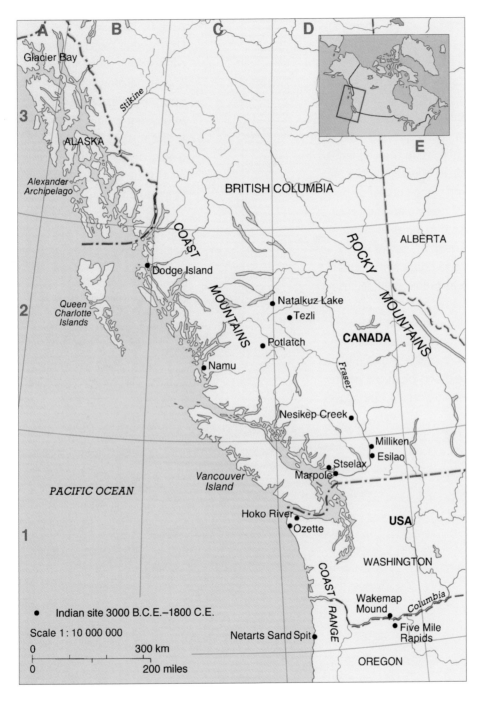

ALASKA

Glacier Bay

Stikine

Alexander
Archipelago

Queen
Charlotte
Islands

BRITISH COLUMBIA

COAST MOUNTAINS

ROCKY MOUNTAINS

ALBERTA

Dodge Island

Natalkuz Lake
Tezli

Potlatch

CANADA

Namu

Fraser

Nesikep Creek

Milliken

Esilao

Vancouver
Island

Stselax
Marpole

PACIFIC OCEAN

Hoko River

Ozette

USA

WASHINGTON

COAST RANGE

Wakemap
Mound

Columbia

Five Mile
Rapids

Netarts Sand Spit

OREGON

• Indian site 3000 B.C.E.–1800 C.E.

Scale 1 : 10 000 000

0   300 km

0   200 miles

gh mountains separated the rocky Pacific coast from the
erior. Here a warm, wet climate has produced a land that
ich in natural resources.

eeded a special harness strapped to his body
order to be able to support the weight.

Potlatches were special feasts that were
ven by people of a high social standing within
the Native American community. Typically,
salmon or seal meat would be served on these
occasions, and gifts would also be handed out
by both the host and the guests. The giving
of gifts at these ceremonies was a method of
demonstrating the social position of both the
giver and the receiver.

MESOAMERICA

Before the Spanish conquerors arrived in Mexico in the 16th century, parts of both Mexico and Central America were settled by different ethnic groups. The area was known as Mesoamerica.

At the end of the Ice Age the climate and landscape of Mesoamerica changed, as it did elsewhere in the Americas. In the highlands of central and southern Mexico, the climate grew drier and warmer, and grasslands became deserts. The herds of grazing animals, such as the mammoth, mastodon, horse, and giant bison, disappeared, and the Native Americans of Mesoamerica had to adapt by hunting smaller game, such as rabbit and deer, using new hunting techniques and tools.

However, hunting was not as vital as elsewhere in the Americas. People likely obtained much food by collecting wild plants and seeds. Even the desert produced edible plants, such as mesquite, cactus, and agave.

Archaic Farming

Over several thousand years, there was a change from gathering plants to growing crop This era is known as the Archaic Period. Exactl how people made the transition from gatherin to growing is not fully understood. One theory is that to save time and the effort of gathering plants, people started to save the seeds and plant extra crop supplies so that they could be sure of a food source.

The earliest cultivated plants looked the same as the wild varieties. Over time, people began to choose seeds from the best plants so

Genetic studies suggest that the Balsas region of Mesoamerica may have been where corn was first grown. The earliest evidence for it comes from dry caves in Oaxaca and Tehuacán. The farmin villages that appeared during the Formative Period (from around 2000 BCE) tended to flourish in more humid areas, such as the Pacific and Gulf coasts, the Maya lowlands, and the fertile highland regions of the Valley of Oaxaca and the Valley of Mexico. Improved varieties of corn and other crops were grown in several areas.

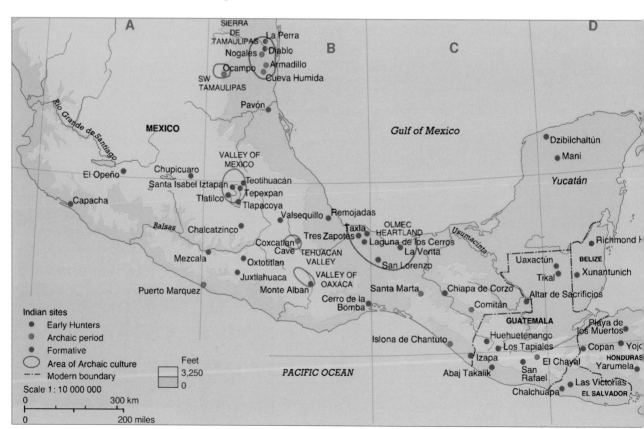

at the new plants produced would be bigger
and better. Plants were not just grown for food.
One of the first plants to be cultivated was a
gourd shaped like a bottle. When the gourd was
hollowed out it made a good storage container.

The Valley of Oaxaca

In present-day central Mexico, the fertile Valley
of Oaxaca played an important role in the
transition from gathering to growing food. The
area is semi-desert and for thousands of years
nomadic hunters and gatherers had camped in
its caves and rock shelters. We know what they
ate, because their food remains have been well
preserved in the dry conditions.

The first crops, grown by 8000 BCE, were
squash and bottle gourds. Corn was also being
grown by about 4300 BCE, but not in large
quantities. Over time, people began to depend
on the food they grew themselves. This led to
them living in settled communities, and moving
around less in search of food. Evidence that
Oaxaca communities were more settled is the
increasing presence of grinding stones used to
prepare corn, as well as the invention of pottery.
This first appeared on Mexico's Pacific coast
about 2500 BCE and spread quickly through
the region. Pots made cooking much easier and

Five thousand years of farming changed the wild corn or maize cob (inset, far left) to the modern cob (inset, far right). The earliest cobs from the Tehuacán Valley were only 1 inch (2.5 cm) long.

also perhaps encouraged people to grow beans
(which were simple to cook in pots). Plant protein
was important in Mesoamerica, as the daily diet
had almost no domesticated animal protein.

The Formative Period

By around 1600 BCE, the first permanent
settlements based on growing food appeared
in Mesoamerica. San José Mogoté in the Valley
of Oaxaca was one of these
settlements. It had a number
of thatched houses with
clay and timber walls. There
may have been about 200
inhabitants, who planted
gardens between the houses.
This time was known as
the Formative Period, when
settled village life became the
normal pattern of living for
Native Americans across
Mesoamerica. Trade also
became more important
between the different
ethnic groups.

Timeline of Mesoamerican Development

THE ARCHAIC PERIOD

c.8000–1000 BCE

c.8000 BCE
Nomadic hunters grew crops, such as squash and bottle gourds, near their campsites.

c.4300 BCE
Corn grown in Valley of Oaxaca.

c.3000 BCE
Villages of pithouses (partly underground dwellings, with wattle and daub sides) formed.

c.2300 BCE
People begin to make pottery.

THE FORMATIVE PERIOD
C.2000 BCE–1 CE (CENTRAL MEXICO) AND C.2000 BCE–290 CE (MAYA HIGHLANDS)

c.1200 BCE
Rise of Olmec civilization.

c.400 BCE
Zapotec city of Monte Albán founded.

c.150 BCE
Rise of the city of Teotihuacan.

THE OLMEC CIVILIZATION

The exact origins of one of the greatest of all the pre-Colombian (the period before the arrival of Christopher Columbus) Mexican civilizations remain a mystery. Archaeologists think that the Olmec civilization probably began as farming settlements based in the fertile river valleys of the modern-day Mexican states of Veracruz and Tabasco. The landscape here is notable for its tropical forests and swamps.

From 1200 BCE, the Olmec civilization began to build large ceremonial centers, of which the most important were at San Lorenzo, La Venta, Laguna de los Cerros, and Tres Zapotes. These centers were distinguished by large earth mounds and huge carved stone monuments.

Stone Carvings

The Olmec civilization is especially notable for the sophistication of its carvings. These ranged from massive stone carvings of what look like human heads and supernatural beings, to small, finely-carved jade pendants. What makes them so amazing is that the Olmec did not have any metal tools with which to carve the stone and semi-precious stones. They most probably carved with chisels and grinding tools made from stone,

Raw Materials Transported to Olmec Centers

Basalt This is a fine-grained dark rock found in volcanoes. It came from the Tuxtla Mountains and the Olmec people used it for monuments, drainage systems, and for making grinding tools.

Obsidian Another volcanic rock, obsidian is dark and glassy. It comes from central Mexico and Guatemala. It was sharp enough to use for making knives and other cutting tools.

Iron Ore This was mined in the Valley of Oaxaca. It was used for making mirrors and jewelry.

Serpentine This rock was greenish black in color and came from the mouth of the Coatzacoalcos River. It was used for making carvings and for jewelry.

Jade This probably came from present-day Honduras and Costa Rica. It was used for making carvings and jewelry.

The Olmec heartland's warm, wet climate produced rich farm land, where corn and other crops grew all year around. Howe many of the raw materials needed by the Olmec people had to acquired through trade with areas outside the heartla.

which would have taken them a lot longer tha working with metal tools.

The stone heads they produced probably represented different Olmec rulers, but most of the carvings that survive are of weird and scary supernatural beings. These were based on creatures from deep in the forests and sea that frightened the Olmec, such as the jaguar, snake, cayman, harpy eagle, and shark. The most important of these beings, and the most frightening, was a half-human, half-animal figure known as a "were-jaguar." This was ofte shown as a howling baby with sharp teeth anc the angry eyes of a growling jaguar.

Trading beyond the Heartland

Many of the raw materials the Olmec needed for their carvings were not found locally. Instead, the Olmec traded with other ethnic

Olmec sculpture ranged from jade objects small enough to be held in the hand, like this one, to huge stone heads that weighed several tons and rested directly on the ground.

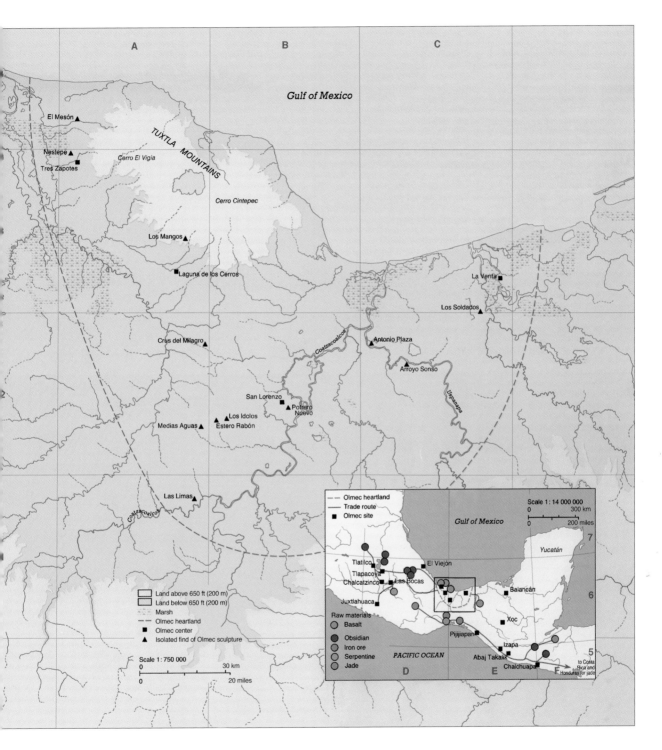

Gulf of Mexico

A   B   C

El Mesón ▲

Nestepe ▲
Tres Zapotes ■

Cerro El Vigia

TUXTLA MOUNTAINS

Cerro Cintepec

Los Mangos ▲

Laguna de los Cerros ■

La Venta ■

Los Soldados ▲

Crus del Milagro ▲

Coatzacoalcos

Antonio Plaza ▲

Arroyo Sonso ▲

Uspanapa

San Lorenzo ■ ▲ Potrero Nuevo

▲ Los Idolos
Medias Aguas ▲ ▲ Estero Rabón

Las Limas ▲

Coatzacoalcos

Land above 650 ft (200 m)
Land below 650 ft (200 m)
Marsh
Olmec heartland
■ Olmec center
▲ Isolated find of Olmec sculpture

Scale 1: 750 000
0   30 km
0   20 miles

Olmec heartland
Trade route
■ Olmec site

Scale 1: 14 000 000
0   300 km
0   200 miles

Gulf of Mexico

Yucatán

Tlatilco
El Viejón
Tlapacoya
Chalcatzinco   Las Bocas
Balancán

Juxtlahuaca

Raw materials
Basalt
Obsidian
Iron ore
Serpentine
Jade

Xoc

Pijijiapan

Izapa
Abaj Takalik
Chalchuapa

to Costa Rica and Honduras for jade

PACIFIC OCEAN

D   E   F

roups. For example, huge basalt boulders from the Tuxtla Mountains were transported to La Venta, probably floated downriver on rafts.

In exchange, the Olmec traded their own goods and these have been found from central Mexico to Costa Rica. Around 400 BCE, the Olmecs started to lose power for reasons that we still do not understand, but their way of life influenced civilizations that later flourished across Mexico, such as the Maya and Aztec.

Mesoamerican Sites

San Lorenzo

One of the most important of all the Olmec sites was the ceremonial center of San Lorenzo. It was built on top of a plateau 165 feet (50 m) high. The

Olmec made the area of the plateau bigger so that they could make their ceremonial center as big as possible. Today, almost 200 earthen mounds can be seen. They are located around rectangular courtyards and were probably used as bases for wooden houses. The larger mounds may have been the bases of temples. The buildings have long since disappeared, because they were made from wood and thatch. There were once a number of artificial pools that may have been used for purification during the religious ceremonies. The Olmecs invented an overflow system of a number of basalt drains that were covered to prevent flooding.

The People of San Lorenzo

San Lorenzo was at its peak between 1200 and 900 BCE. The massive carved stone heads found at the site probably represented the local rulers. At its peak, San Lorenzo may have had 1000 important members of its community living there, chiefly the rulers, nobles, and priests. The rest of the community, perhaps numbering around 2000, would have lived at lower levels in farming villages.

Around 900 BCE, ceremonial life in San Lorenzo came to a sudden end when the center

Colossal stone heads have been found at both San Lorenzo and La Venta: They may be portraits of Olmec rulers.

as deliberately destroyed. Stone sculptures ere smashed up and the pieces of stone were ried. Although people seem to have carried living there for some time, no new onuments were erected.

Venta

San Lorenzo's power came to an end, La nta rose to take its place. La Venta became e main political and religious center of the gion. Located in the swamps of what is now orthern Tabasco is a group of earthen mounds.

The largest mound at La Venta is known the Great Pyramid. It is more than 100 feet 0 m) high with a base that measures 420 et (130 m) across. To the north of the Great ramid are a number of lower mounds and urtyards. Archaeologists have found burial sites with rich grave goods still in them under some of these mounds. Since the soil is acidic, any human remains have disappeared.

Ceremonial Burial Offerings

People at La Venta buried offerings. Experts have excavated mirrors made from polished iron ore, axheads, necklaces, and small figurines made from jade, serpentine, and granite. The most spectacular find was three mosaic pavements, each made from 485 serpentine blocks that show the face of a jaguar.

Just as at San Lorenzo, La Venta was suddenly and deliberately destroyed around 400 BCE. Its monuments were also defaced, but nobody knows why this happened.

These figurines were buried in a careful arrangement beneath a floor at La Venta: They may be representing a ceremony.

Teotihuacán

Located about 30 miles (48 km) northeast of Mexico City, lie the remains of Teotihuacán, the greatest of all the ancient American

cities. Occupying more than 8 square miles (20 sq km), it was laid out on a rectangular grid pattern, thousands of years before New York City was designed in a similar way. The city of Teotihuacán consisted of temples, palaces, and houses, and was home to as many as 125,000 people. The size of the city reflected its power. Over a period of hundreds of years, the city dominated the Valley of Mexico, and its influence reached far and wide throughout much of Mesoamerica.

The main street of Teotihuacán is the so-called "Avenue of the Dead," which crosses the center of the city in a north–south direction. Along the Avenue of the Dead are the ruins of

The Pyramid of the Moon rises behind a sculpted head on a temple in Teotihuacán. Archaeologists have discovered human and animal sacrifices buried within the pyramid.

more than 75 temples. The largest of these is also the oldest temple, the "Pyramid of the Sun." Archaeologists have discovered that the pyramid was built over a secret cave. The carvings and paintings on the pyramid clearly show images of gods that were also worshipped by later civilizations, such as Tlaloc (the Rain God) and Quetzalcoatl (the Feathered Serpent).

There is still much to be learned about the people of Teotihuacán. For example, modern-day archaeologists are only now beginning to realize that the Teotihuacán civilization used writing in a similar way to other important Mesoamerican civilizations, such as the Maya.

A Great Center of Trade and Craft

Teotihuacán was a large center for craftsmen. There were hundreds of workshops throughout the city. Craftsmen made tools and weapons from obsidian, which were traded with other groups, and they also carved ornaments from imported shells and jade. Other craftsmen made pottery that varied from heavy pots for cooking to delicate vases and incense burners. These goods were traded across Mesoamerica.

Merchants traded the goods that were made at Teotihuacán for raw materials found elsewhere in Mesoamerica. They brought back turquoise from southwestern North America; shells and copal incense came from the Gulf Coast; and the Maya supplied quetzal feathers. Archaeological evidence suggests that merchants from Teotihuacán may have lived in Maya cities, where they not only traded, but also married into the local community.

Around 500–550 CE, much of Teotihuacán was abandoned after it was largely destroyed by fire. Its destruction was the result of internal squabbles rather than caused by attacks from enemies. Although the city was no longer the magnificent and important center it had once been, its significance was not forgotten. The mighty Aztec emperors made pilgrimages to its temples almost 1,000 years later.

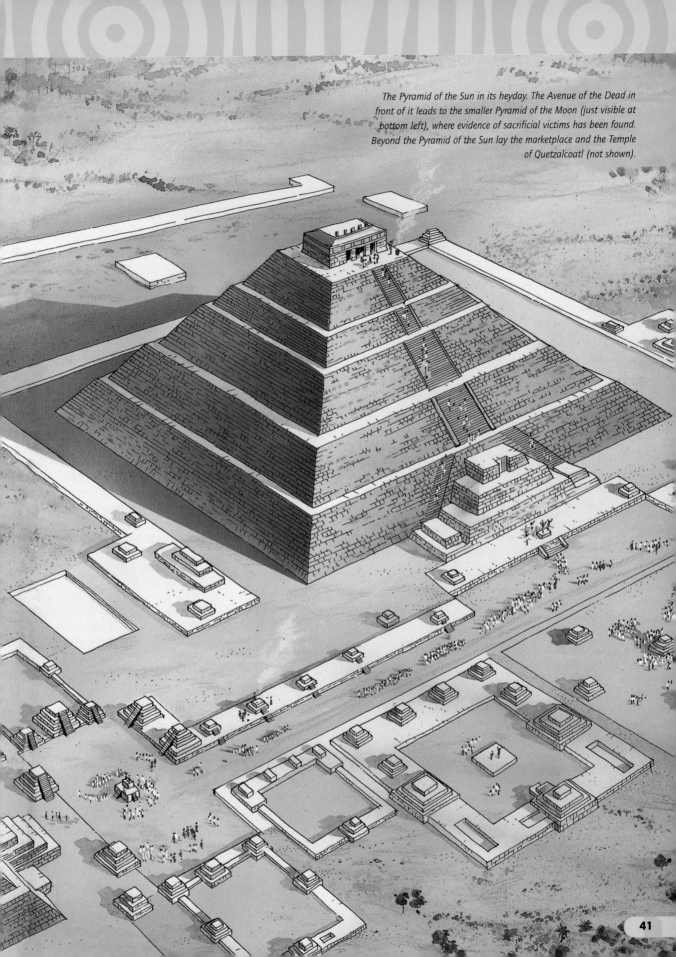

The Pyramid of the Sun in its heyday. The Avenue of the Dead in front of it leads to the smaller Pyramid of the Moon (just visible at bottom left), where evidence of sacrificial victims has been found. Beyond the Pyramid of the Sun lay the marketplace and the Temple of Quetzalcoatl (not shown).

MAYA CIVILIZATION

The greatest of all the Mesoamerican civilizations was that of the Maya. It was credited with inventing many things, including the astronomical calendar. The Maya practised agriculture, constructed great stone buildings and pyramid temples, worked with gold and copper, and used a form of hieroglyphic writing that they may have learned from the Olmecs.

The magnificent stone cities that the Maya built were, over the passage of time, lost to the jungles of Mexico and Central America, but many of these cities, with their spectacular temple-pyramids and palaces, have now been rediscovered and partially restored to give a glimpse of their former splendor.

City-States and Warrior Kings

Each Maya city was an independent state with its own king. The royal dynasty was usually male, with succession passing from father to eldest son. The king was an absolute ruler who claimed to be descended from the gods. It was normal for the king to inscribe his family tree onto the walls of the impressive monuments he had built to honor his rule.

The Maya c.300 BCE–1541 CE

c.300 BCE–300 CE The early Maya people were influenced by the further reaches of the Olmec civilization at Izapa, Abaj Takalik, El Baúl, and Kaminalijuyu. The Maya build ceremonial centers in the southern lowlands, such as Tikal, Uaxactún, and El Mirador.

300–800 CE The golden age of Maya civilization. Architecture, art, and science all flourish in magnificent cities, such as Copán, Quiriguá, Naranjo, Piedras Negras, Uxmal, Cobá, and Chichén Itzá.

800–900 CE Maya civilization in the southern lowlands collapses for reasons that are still unclear. Many cities are abandoned.

c.980 CE Toltecs invade Yucatán and make Chichén Itzá their capital. The Maya civilization survives under Toltec rule.

1200–1500 CE New Maya capital established at Mayapan. Decline of Maya civilization.

1517–1541 CE Spanish conquest of Guatemala and Yucatán.

The city-states spent much of their time at war. They did not just want to win territory from their neighbors, but they also wanted prisoners. These prisoners were used as human sacrifices during important religious ceremonies.

Time and Astrology

The concept of time was very important to the Maya, because they wanted to record the continuing family tree that linked the gods to their present ruler. With this in mind, the Maya invented a system of recording time, which was known as the Long Count. This worked by counting the number of days that had passed since a certain starting point. The date they chose as their starting point corresponds to the year 3114 BCE in our calendar. We still don't know why the Maya chose that date.

The Maya had two calendars. One was a sacred calendar and the other was a daily calendar. The daily calendar had 365 days (like ours), which were divided into 18 months

The Maya did not have an alphabet. They wrote in pictures, or "glyphs". Most Maya inscriptions concern important events in the lives of Maya rulers. The scene shown below is carved on a stone lintel found at Yaxchilán. The top and middle glyphs tell how, on a certain day, Bird Jaguar, the ruler of Yaxchilán, took two important prisoners. The prisoners' names are written on their thighs.

(on) 7 Imix 14 Tzec chucha "(he) was captured"

Jeweled skull

"captor of"

second captive

u bac "the captive of"

Bird Jaguar Lord of Yaxchilá

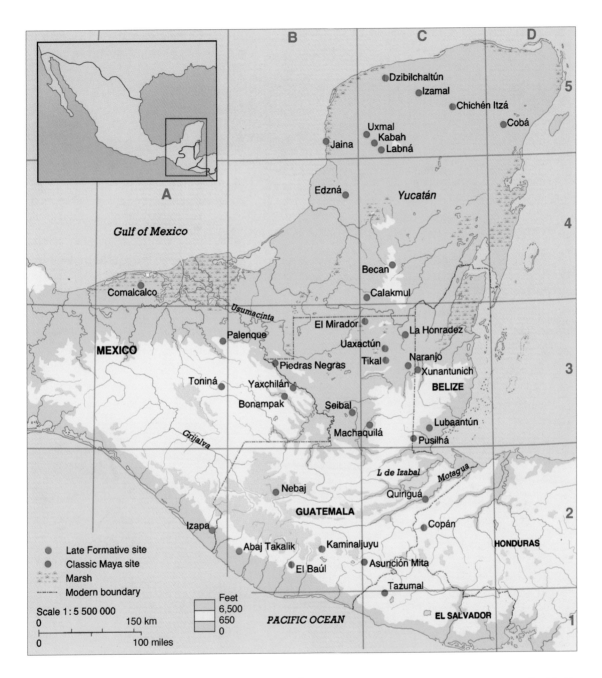

The map shows the following labeled sites and features:

- **Dzibilchaltún**
- **Izamal**
- **Chichén Itzá**
- **Cobá**
- **Uxmal**
- **Kabah**
- **Jaina**
- **Labná**
- **Edzná**
- **Yucatán**
- **Gulf of Mexico**
- **Becan**
- **Calakmul**
- **Comalcalco**
- **Usumacinta**
- **El Mirador**
- **La Honradez**
- **Palenque**
- **Uaxactún**
- **Naranjo**
- **MEXICO**
- **Piedras Negras**
- **Tikal**
- **Xunantunich**
- **Toniná**
- **Yaxchilán**
- **BELIZE**
- **Bonampak**
- **Seibal**
- **Lubaantún**
- **Machaquilá**
- **Pusilhá**
- **Grijalva**
- **L. de Izabal**
- **Motagua**
- **Nebaj**
- **Quiriguá**
- **GUATEMALA**
- **Izapa**
- **Copán**
- **Abaj Takalik**
- **Kaminaljuyu**
- **HONDURAS**
- **El Baúl**
- **Asunción Mita**
- **Tazumal**
- **EL SALVADOR**
- **PACIFIC OCEAN**

Legend:
- ● Late Formative site
- ● Classic Maya site
- Marsh
- Modern boundary

Scale 1 : 5 500 000
0 — 150 km
0 — 100 miles

Feet
6,500
650
0

20 days each, with an extra five days at the
end. The sacred calendar consisted of 260 days,
which were divided into 13 weeks of 20 days.
This calendar was used to predict the future
and to avoid bad luck.

Only priests who had trained in astrology
were allowed to read the sacred calendar, and
people asked for their advice before important
events. For example, if a child was born on what

For more than 500 years, Maya civilization flourished in three regions: in the highlands of Guatemala; in the low-lying tropical rain forests of northern Guatemala and Belize; and in the Yucatán peninsula. Most Maya cities were independent states, although their rulers were often linked by marriage.

was considered to be an unlucky day by
the sacred calendar, the child's naming day
ceremony was set for a lucky day to help to
bring the infant good luck.

Palenque

Lying on the most westerly edge of the Maya empire was the city-state of Palenque. Today, it is located in the Mexican state of Chiapas, set among the forested foothills that overlook the coastal plain that stretches all the way to the Gulf of Mexico.

Palenque was a small and insignificant state until about 600 CE. Then, in 615 CE, a new ruler, aged only 12 years, ascended to the throne. His name was Pacal, and his reign transformed the fortunes of Palenque. During his long reign, and the reigns of his two sons, Chan-Bahlum and Kan-Xul II, the city grew into a large and powerful center that controlled the surrounding area.

Pacal's Tomb

The wealth and importance of Palenque is clear to see from its beautifully decorated buildings. Many were adorned with painted plasterwork or stucco that was brightly colored. One of the most magnificent of all Palenque's buildings is the "Temple of the Inscriptions". Pacal built the temple to house his tomb. It sits on top of a nine-tiered pyramid, because, according to Maya mythology, the underworld had nine levels. It is thought that each tier of the pyramid was meant to represent one of these levels.

Stone panels in the temple are intricately carved with "glyphs" (picture carvings) that

ow human and animal forms, as well as long
d complex inscriptions in hieroglyphics that
ld the story of Pacal's life and ancestry.

   When Pacal died in 683 CE at the age
 80, he was buried in a stone sarcophagus
eneath the base of the pyramid. The lid of
e sarcophagus was carved with pictures that
ow Pacal entering the underworld. The walls
 Pacal's tomb were decorated with stucco
nels that depict the nine "Lords of the Night",
ho ruled the underworld.

e Palenque Palace

alenque continued to prosper under the rule of
cal's sons. They were responsible for building
veral new temples. The palace was made
gger and a four-story tower was added. This
as unique in Maya architecture. The palace

even had its own water supply. The water was
transported via a stone-lined aqueduct from the
Otulum River close to the palace.

   Archeologists are unsure as to the exact use
of the palace. They think that it may have been
used as a ceremonial center rather than a royal
residence, because some of the wall decorations
show ceremonies that may have taken place
there, such as the crowning of Maya rulers. The
images give a good idea of just how luxurious
court life was. Other images focus on warfare
and show rows of prisoners, indicating just how
important warfare was to the Maya. In fact,
warfare may have been the cause of the
Maya's final downfall in the 9th century CE.

*The ceremonial center at the ancient Maya city of Palenque,
with the Temple of Inscriptions on the left atop the pyramid,
and the palace, complete with its tower, on the right.*

THE TOLTECS

Where the Toltecs came from remains a mystery. They most probably were made up of a mixture of different groups, including the Tolteca-Chichimeca and the Tolteca-Nonoalca. The Tolteca-Chichimeca was an aggressive clan of hunter-gatherers who lived in the rocky desert of northern Mexico. While they lived principally as nomads, they may also have practiced some farming. The other group, the Tolteca-Nonoalca, originated from further south. They are thought to have been skilled sculptors and craftsmen who probably helped to build the magnificent city of Tula.

The mighty Aztecs claimed to be the direct descendants of the Toltecs and described them in glowing terms:

"The Toltecs were wise. Their works were all good, all perfect, all wonderful, all marvelous; their houses beautiful, tiled in mosaics, stuccoed, smoothed, very marvelous... they were thinkers, for they originated the year count, the day count; they established the way in which the night, the day, would work."

Archaeologists do not agree with the Aztecs' generous view of the Toltecs. The archaeological evidence proves that the Toltec were not, in fact, a peace-loving people, but fierce and warlike. During the 11th and 12th centuries CE they ruled central Mexico by force and they often fought amongst themselves.

The City of Tula

Tula was the Toltec capital. It was built on a ridge about 40 miles (65 km) northwest of modern-day Mexico City, overlooking a vast valley. Archaeologists have found evidence of the warlike nature of the Toltecs at Tula. As well as painted reliefs and statues of warriors, there

The Toltecs were a mixture of nomadic tribes from the Chichimec Desert and Nonoalca people from the modern state of Oaxaca ar the Gulf Coast. During the 10th and 11th centuries CE, they sprer into many parts of Mesoamerica.

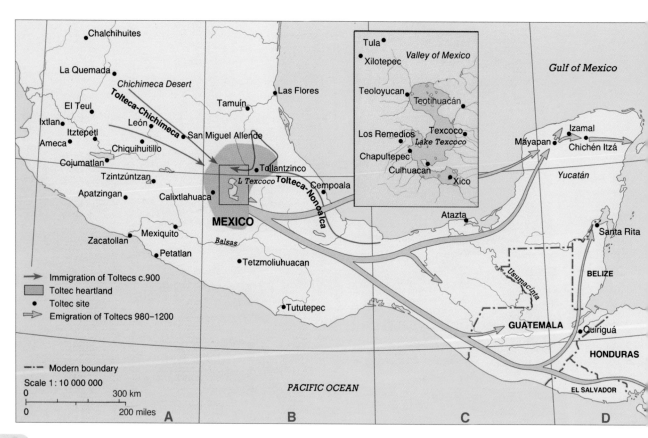

One distinctive feature of Tula was the strange stone figures called Chac Mools. They were found in the temple and other parts of the city. These figures were carved in the shape of warriors and were lying on their backs. Bowls that were carved onto their chests indicate that the Chac Mools were used during sacrifices. It may be that the hearts or blood of the victims were placed in the bowls.

The Destruction of Tula

Nomads from the northern desert attacked Tula in 1168 CE. They destroyed much of the city, looting temples and palaces, and pushing the great stone warriors to the ground. The Toltecs fled, leaving the city in ruins and abandoned. Today, little remains of the huge immense ceremonial platform with its serpent columns.

The Toltec occupation of Tula lasted for about 200 years, but the Toltecs' belief in worshipping the sun, and their society's warlike nature, survived in the Aztec empire.

e other war-related images. These include rvings of skulls and crossbones, serpents allowing skeletons, eagles eating hearts, and rowling jaguars and coyotes. Centuries later, agles, jaguars, and coyotes were symbols of e elite warriors of the Aztec empire.

At its peak, Tula was magnificent. Its nterpiece was the four-tiered temple-pyramid low known to archaeologists as Pyramid B). hen visitors arrived at the temple, they would alk through a hall with columns that were ecorated with carvings of marching warriors. one pillars carved in the shape of feathered rpents surrounded the doorway to the temple. e temple roof was supported by the heads of ur massive stone warriors.

Rise and Fall of the Toltecs

c.900 CE Chichimeca nomads arrive in the Valley of Mexico.

c.950 CE The Chichimeca join forces with the Nonoalca people, who came from the south to found the city of Tula.

c.1000 CE The Maya city of Chichén Itzá was taken over, perhaps by the Toltecs from Tula (according to Maya texts.)

1168 CE Tula was destroyed by nomadic invaders.

c.1200 CE The power of Chichén Itzá declines. The Maya build a new capital city at Mayapan.

Chichén Itzá

Probably the most spectacular of all of the known ancient Mesoamerican ruins are those of Chichén Itzá in the Yucatán Peninsula. At its peak, Chichén Itzá was one of the most important of all the Maya cities. However, by the 13th century CE, its power had declined.

Chichén Itzá was controlled by different groups throughout its history. After the Spanish conquest of Mexico in the 16th century CE, Spanish chroniclers wrote down the history of the region, as related to them by the Aztecs and others. The first Bishop of Yucatán, Diego de Landa, writing about Chichén Itzá, said:

"It is believed among the Indians that with the Itzas who occupied Chichén Itzá, there reigned a great lord named Kukulcan ... They say that he arrived from the west ... he was regarded in Mexico as one of their gods and called Quetzalcoatl; and they also

The massive Pyramid of Kukulcan, or Quetzalcoatl, at Chichén Itzá. Known as the Castillo in Spanish, this is a pyramid built on nine tiers, with a temple on the top.

considered him a god in Yucatán on account of his being a just statesman."

The Aztec people believed that Topiltzin Quetzalcoatl was a wise and peace-loving king who once ruled the Toltec city of Tula. When a fierce warlike god, Tezcatlipoca, challenged his position, Quetzalcoatl was forced to flee from Tula. According to legend, he sailed across the Gulf of Mexico on a raft made from serpents, promising to return one day to reclaim his rightful position. This is the same Quetzalcoatl that was worshipped at Chichén Itzá.

The most spectacular of all the buildings at Chichén Itzá is the Castillo (castle), which is located in the center of the main plaza. In fact, it is not a castle, but a pyramid-shaped temple dedicated to Quetzalcoatl. When the site was excavated in the 1930s, archaeologist discovered that it had been built over an earlie temple-pyramid. One theory is that the first pyramid was actually a royal tomb.

The "Well of Sacrifice"

An interesting feature of the Yucatán Peninsula is the natural wells, or "cenotes,"

at dot the landscape. At Chichén Itzá, a useway led to the Sacred Cenote, which was dicated to the rain god. The well remained site of pilgrimage long after the Spanish onquest. In 1900 CE the Sacred Cenote as dredged. All kinds of interesting offerings ere found. They included copal incense, rved jade, and decorated gold discs. Human ones found in the cenote prove that human crifice took place.

e Great Ballcourt

kind of ballgame, "tlachti", was very popular ross Mesoamerica. The game was played on specially-built ballcourt by two teams who ed to knock a large, solid rubber ball through stone ring. It was a kind of early version of odern-day basketball.

The Great Ballcourt at Chichén Itzá is the rgest of all the known ancient ballcourts. It easures 480 feet (146 m) long and 120 feet 7 m) wide, which is about the same size as a odern soccer field. The oldest ballcourt so far

discovered by archaeologists is in Chiapas, Mexico, and dates back to about 1700 BCE.

Chichén Itzá's ballcourt was especially difficult to play on. The stone rings were set high on the court wall, about 26 feet (8 m) above the court floor. Players were not allowed to touch the ball with their hands, only with their hips and knees. They wore protective clothing that included a heavy belt made from wood and leather, leather hip pads, kneepads, and gloves.

It was not unusual for players to be badly injured or even to be killed while playing the game, as it was so rough. The game was often literally a matter of life and death, because the defeated opponent was often sacrificed after the game. Carvings around the walls of the Great Ballcourt show members of the winning team beheading a defeated opponent. The games were avidly watched by large crowds of spectators who lined up on each side of the ballcourt. They cheered on their team and bet on which team might win.

THE AZTEC EMPIRE

The Aztec Empire was one of the greatest of all the Mesoamerican cultures and, at its peak, it dominated a vast area that stretched from the Pacific coast to the border with Guatemala.

The Aztec people believed that they were the descendants of nomads from northern Mexico. They arrived at Lake Texcoco in the Valley of Mexico about 1300 CE, guided by their chief god, Huitzilopochtli. The valley was already occupied by powerful city-states and for some time the Aztecs worked as slaves for the rulers.

In 1345 CE, the Aztecs settled on swampy islands on the western bank of Lake Texcoco. They believed in a prophecy that they would build a magnificent city on the site where they saw an eagle with a snake in its mouth sitting on top of a prickly pear cactus. When the Azte[c] saw the eagle, serpent, and cactus, they did not allow the unfavorable landscape to stop them. They learned to reclaim land from the swamp, and built houses made from thatch and cane and a temple to Huitzilopochtli. They named the place Tenochtitlán ("place of the prickly pear cactus").

The Aztecs were fierce warriors and they increased their power by working as soldiers fo[r] the neighboring city-state of Atzcapotzalco. Eventually they became so strong that they conquered Atzcapotzalco and took control of [its] lands. After they formed the Triple Alliance (a[n] alliance between the three most important Aztec city-states), their power grew quickly. In a period of less than 200 years, the Aztecs controlled an empire of some 10 million peopl[e].

The Aztec Army

At the heart of the Aztec expansion was their well-organized and well-equipped army. The Aztec Army was divided into units under the control of officers, who earned their positions by merit and not by birth. Some were elected [by] their soldiers, while others showed their prowe[ss] by taking prisoners during battle. The prisoner[s] were needed for use as human sacrifices in the many ceremonies the Aztecs held each year. T[he]

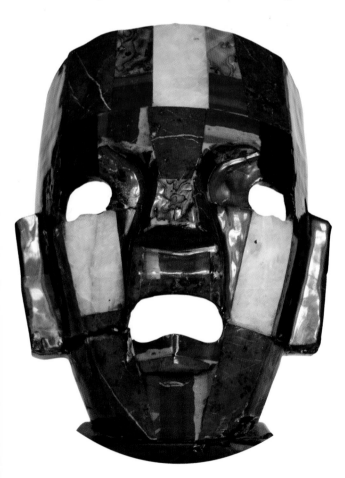

Masks made from gold or precious or semiprecious stones were so important in rituals that they were part of the tribute paid to the Aztecs by conquered peoples in their empire.

The Aztec Empire 1345–1521 CE

1345 CE The Aztecs establish Tenochtitlán on Lake Texcoco.

1428 CE Triple Alliance formed (Texcoco, Tenochtitlán, and Tlacopán). The Aztecs take control of the Valley of Mexico.

1440–1468 CE Emperor Montezuma I expands the Aztec Empire to the Gulf of Mexico.

1486–1502 CE Emperor Ahuizotl expands the Aztec Empire to the Pacific coast and south to the Guatemalan border.

1519 CE Spanish invaders land in Mexico.

1520–1521 CE Emperor Montezuma II killed. End of the Aztec Empire.

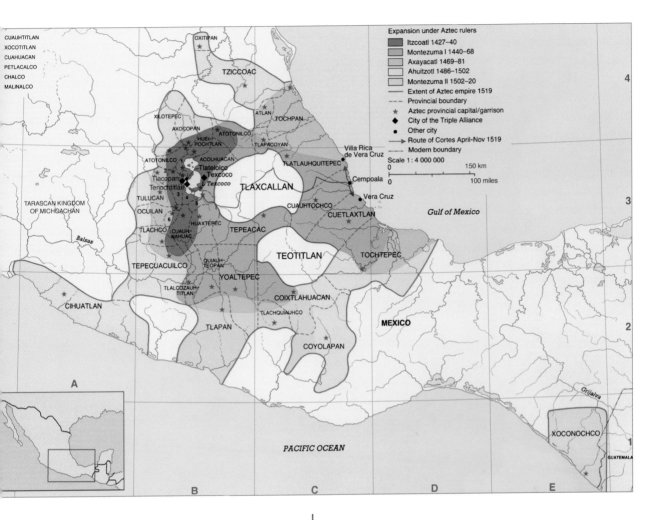

The following labels appear on the map:

CUAUHTITLAN
XOCOTITLAN
CUAHUACAN
PETLACALCO
CHALCO
MALINALCO

OXITIPAN

TZICCOAC

XILOTEPEC
AXOCOPAN
ATOTONILCO
HUEI-POCHTLAN
ATLAN
TOCHPAN
TLAPACOYAN

ATOTONILCO
ACOLHUACAN
Tlatelolco
Texcoco
Tlacopan
Texcoco
Tenochtitlán
TULUCAN
OCUILAN
TLACHCO
CUAUH-NAHUAC
HUAXTEPEC
TEPEACAC
TLATLAUHQUITEPEC
CUAUHTOCHCO
CUETLAXTLAN

Villa Rica de Vera Cruz
Cempoala
Vera Cruz

TLAXCALLAN

TARASCAN KINGDOM OF MICHOACÁN
Balsas

TEOTITLAN
TOCHTEPEC

Gulf of Mexico

TEPECUACUILCO
QUIAUH-TEOPAN
YOALTEPEC
TLALCOZAUH-TITLAN
CIHUATLAN
TLAPAN
COIXTLAHUACAN
TLACHQUIAUHCO
COYOLAPAN

MEXICO

PACIFIC OCEAN

Grijalva

XOCONOCHCO

GUATEMALA

Expansion under Aztec rulers
- Itzcoatl 1427–40
- Montezuma I 1440–68
- Axayacatl 1469–81
- Ahuitzotl 1486–1502
- Montezuma II 1502–20
- Extent of Aztec empire 1519
- Provincial boundary
- ★ Aztec provincial capital/garrison
- ◆ City of the Triple Alliance
- ● Other city
- → Route of Cortes April–Nov 1519
- Modern boundary

Scale 1 : 4 000 000
0   150 km
0   100 miles

By 1502 CE the Aztec Empire had reached its full extent. Teotitlán, Tlaxcallan, and the Tarascan kingdom stayed as independent states. Conquered provinces had to pay an annual tribute to the empire, such as food or luxury goods, such as jaguar skins and quetzal feathers.

"Flowery Wars" were battles arranged with other states with the intention of capturing prisoners for use as sacrificial victims.

All Aztec boys above 15 years of age were trained as warriors, unless they trained to be priests. Each warrior wore a tunic of quilted cotton and carried a shield. Higher-ranking Aztec soldiers wore carved wooden helmets, animal skins, or feather costumes. Weapons included the spear and spear thrower ("atlatl"), slings, and bows and arrows. The "macahuitl" was a flat club edged with blades of obsidian.

The Aztec Emperor

The emperor of the Aztecs was elected. He came from the royal family and was voted into his position by a council of nobles, priests, and warriors. Once elected, he was given the title of "Tlatoani," which means "Speaker."

We know most about the last Aztec emperor, Montezuma II, who was defeated by the Spanish conquerors in the 16th century CE. Spanish chroniclers wrote about how the Aztec emperor was treated like a god. Nobody was permitted to look him in the face and he was always carried in a litter, so that his feet never touched the ground. Cloths were also put down to prevent his feet from making contact with the earth. Anyone approaching the ruler had to be barefoot and had to bow their heads.

The Aztec Capital

When the Spanish first saw the Aztec capital city, Tenochtitlán, they could not believe their eyes. One Spanish chronicler, Bernal Diaz, wrote about his first sighting of the place in 1519 CE:

"When we saw so many cities and villages built both on the water and on dry land ... we could not resist our admiration ... because of the high towers, cues [pyramids] and other buildings, all of masonry, which rose from the water. Some of our soldiers asked if [it] was not a dream."

Tenochtitlán had been built on swampy islands in Lake Texcoco. It had grown into a rich and powerful city of more than half a million people. Spanish scribes described at length the busy city, with its towering temple and palaces where people thronged to the thriving markets, and where the suburbs were full of homes and gardens. One of the most distinctive of all the features of the city was its floating gardens, or "chinampas." These were ingenious plant beds made from bamboo that were used to grow fruit and vegetables.

The Great Market at Tenochtitlán
The incredible variety of produce available at Tenochtitlán's market showed just how wealthy

e Aztec capital had become. Goods were ansported from all over the Aztec Empire to be aded at the market. The goods were brought Tenochtitlán on canoes that crowded the ty's vast network of canals. Every day more an 60,000 people came to the marketplace order to trade. As well as food and clothes, Il kinds of other goods were for sale. Pottery ups and dishes, tobacco pipes, and cigarettes ere popular. Luxury goods included precious etals, like gold and silver, and semi-precious ones, such as jade, as well as exotic bird eathers. Slaves were also traded. They were isplayed for sale in wooden cages.

Since the Aztecs did not use money, they mostly bartered for goods. However, there were some fixed units of exchange that everyone used. For example, cocoa beans were used as a way of giving small change, while a jade necklace or a woven mantle, or cloak, was considered to be very valuable. A mantle was traded as the equivalent of 100 cocoa beans.

Aztec nobles and warriors survey the ceremonial center of Tenochtitlán. The temple of Quetzalcoatl is before them, and beyond it is the great double temple-pyramid dedicated to Huitzilopochtli, the God of War, and Tlaloc, the Rain God. Nearby (right) is the "tzompantli", or skull rack, where the heads of sacrificial victims were put on display. In the distance are groups of houses and gardens.

THE CENTRAL ANDES

The Central Andes region is what we know today as northern and central Peru in South America. The mighty Andes Mountains formed a massive natural barrier for the earliest inhabitants of the region, who hunted animals and also collected wild plants. Eventually, these people turned to fishing the rich waters of the Pacific Ocean, and started to farm. They made their fishing nets from cotton twine and used hollowed-out gourds for their floats.

Crops were quite varied. The early farmers grew squash, beans, chilli peppers, potatoes, and corn, which had been introduced from Mesoamerica. They had dogs, which they kept as pets and for hunting. They raised ducks and guinea pigs to eat. The early inhabitants kept herds of llamas and alpacas to provide wool to be woven into clothing and for meat. The llamas were also used to transport goods. Today the descendants of these early people still use alpacas and llamas.

The region was home to several of the greatest of all the New World civilizations. Both the Moche and Chimu people lived along the coastline, while the Inca were based in the highlands. Each civilization borrowed much from those that had existed before them. For example, after the Inca conquered the Chimu around 1470 CE, they absorbed Chimu art and culture into their own civilization.

The Chavín Civilization

Around 3000 BCE people began to build large ceremonial complexes along Peru's desert coast. They were able to settle in fixed communities because of the abundance of fish in the ocean, which fed them. Much later, between 400 and 200 BCE, the site at Chavín de Huantar, in what is now Peru, began to flourish. The people who lived there developed a unique style of art, religious beliefs, and advances in textile and metal production that spread across the region to much of Peru.

At the heart of the Chavín de Huantar site was a large temple. It consisted of numerous small rooms and passages connected together by stairways. Archaeologists think it was most likely a center of pilgrimage for people who traveled there from other parts of the region.

The peaks in the central Andes are so high that they are permanently covered in snow. The early peoples of the region followed pathways and passes among the mountains that are still used for transportation today.

ombs at Paracas

large number of tombs have been found on
ie Paracas peninsula. They date from between
00 and 200 BCE and are especially notable
r their good state of preservation. The dry
esert preserved the tombs, which contained
ummified bodies wrapped in layers of cloth.
ie layers were made up from cotton clothes,
ich as shirts, mantles, loincloths, and turbans
r the head. Many of the clothes were
nbellished with beautiful embroidery, which
epicted strange mythical beasts, birds, and
nimals. We can even tell what color the wool
as, because the dry desert air has preserved
ie material so well.

etalworking in the Andes

etalworking was an important industry in
ie Andes region of the Americas. For the
ica, gold and silver were the most precious
f metals. The Spanish conquerors said that
ie Inca thought of gold as "the sweat of the
in" and silver as "the tears of the moon." The
arliest known metalwork to have so far been
iscovered dates back to about 1500 BCE and

*The Native Americans obtained most of their gold by panning in
highland streams and rivers. They used "digging sticks" (straight,
pointed sticks) to loosen and break up the earth and gravel, which
they then washed in shallow wooden trays. In some areas, they
also dug shafts to mine veins of quartz to extract gold. Silver and
copper ores were dug from pits and then smelted in clay furnaces.
Copper and bronze were used to make weapons and tools, while
gold and silver were mainly for jewelry and ceremonial objects.*

consists of simply a few pieces of gold foil.
Later, gold, silver, copper, and even platinum
were all mined and worked. These materials
were often mixed with other metals to form
alloys. In particular, copper was mixed with tin
to make bronze, which became an important
metal for the Inca people. Smiths prepared the
metal by hammering it into thin sheets. Then,
various shapes were cut to make masks, crowns,
ear ornaments, necklaces, and pins. Human and
animal figures were also cast in molds and were
particularly valuable.

It was the discovery of the plentiful gold
and silver riches of the Americas that inspired
the Spaniards to conquer the continent. This
made Spain the richest country in the world in
the 16th century CE.

Central Andean Sites

On the northern coast of present-day Peru, near the modern city of Trujillo, stands the ancient site of Moche. Between the 2nd and 8th centuries CE the Moche civilization thrived here. The Moche people were very technologically advanced. They were farmers who grew a wide variety of crops, and to irrigate these crops they constructed an impressive system of canals and aqueducts, many of which were great feats of engineering. In order to trade with other Native American peoples, the Moche also built reed boats to transport their goods by means of the canal networks, and also for use on the sea.

The dry, desert climate of northern Peru has greatly helped modern archaeologists to discover more about how the Moche lived, because many Moche artefacts have been preserved by the dry conditions. Pottery found in Moche tombs was highly decorated and a great deal of this painted decoration has survived. It shows the daily activities of the Moche, such as hunting, fishing, and weaving, as well as the gods, rituals, and ceremonies that were revered by Moche civilization.

Temples and Pyramids

The Moche also built large temples. The two great pyramid-shaped temples—the Huaca del Sol ("Temple of the Sun") and the Huaca de la Luna ("Temple of the Moon")—at the site of Moche are probably the best examples of their architecture. The Temple of the Sun (a name given to the building by the Spanish) is the larger of the two temples, and has a terraced pyramid on its top. It is probably the largest adobe building in the Americas. Today, it stands about 130 feet (40 m) high and is about 1,150 feet (350 m) long, but it was almost certainly once much bigger. Archaeologists believe that it was constructed over a period of several

centuries. The final addition to the building contained the graves of two people, but the structure was not originally built as a tomb. The Temple of the Moon (also a name given by the Spanish) sits at the foot of the Cerro Blanco hil It consists of several rooms and courtyards, and it rises to a height of about 70 feet (21 m).

It is highly probable that both of these temples were used for religious ceremonies. Archaeologists think this because some of the detail on Moche pottery shows prisoners being sacrificed on top of pyramids.

Tiwanaku and Wari

The Tiwanaku and Wari civilizations came to prominence in much of the central and southern Andes and along the coast between 650 and 1000 CE. Tiwanaku (Tiahuanaco) is the name given to ruins that lie on a vast blea plateau (known as the "altiplano") outside La Paz, the capital city of modern Bolivia. This is around 13 miles (20 km) east of the vast landlocked Lake Titicaca, the highest navigable lake in the world, which forms part of the present-day border between Bolivia and Peru.

Despite the dusty and treeless appearance of the plateau, Native American people have occupied this area for several thousand years, because it is the largest area of flat farming land to be found in the Andes. Crops such as potatoes and quinoa (a grain) could grow here, and the land was good for grazing llamas and alpaca. The mountains provided a rich source of gold, silver, copper, and tin.

Tiwanaku, Akapana, and Kalasasaya

This was almost certainly a ceremonial center, suggested by the ruins of large stone buildings. The biggest structures are the Akapana, a large terraced pyramid, and the Kalasasaya, a great temple enclosure. Located in the northwest corner of the Kalasasaya is the best known of all the ruins at the Tiwanaku site, the so-called "Gateway of the Sun." The gateway is about feet (3 m) high, and is carved from a single ock of stone. At its top is a carved depiction f a human figure wearing a headdress of uma heads. On the figure's body are condor nd puma heads, and human faces hang from s belt. These may have been the heads of acrificial victims!

odels for the Inca

he Wari people (also known as the Huari) lived the southern highlands of Peru, close to the odern-day city of Ayachucho. There is some milarity between the stone carvings and the ottery found here and those discovered in

Tiwanaku, although those of the Wari are less elaborate in form. However, the similarities between the carvings suggest that the two civilizations were in contact with one another, despite their main centers being about 400 miles (600 km) apart. Both expanded their empires at about the same time, and the organization of their empires was similar. Both civilizations served as models for the Inca state.

A fishing boat on the waters of Lake Titicaca. The vessel is known as a "balsa" and is based on an ancient design. The boat is made from bundles of reeds that are bound together. Sails are made of cotton or of woven reed matting. The people of Tiwanaku used similar boats before the Spanish Conquest.

THE INCA

The Inca rose from a small group living in the southern Andes to become one of the mightiest empires of the Americas. They built an empire through conquest and ran it through highly administration. Over a period of less than a century, between 1440 CE and the arrival of the Spanish conquerors in the Inca empire in 1532 CE, the Inca became the most powerful group in the region. Under Pachacuti, the Inca ruler, they expanded aggressively and very rapidly until their empire stretched almost 2,500 miles (4,000 km) along the western coast of South America, from northern Ecuador to central Chile.

Conquered Territories

When the Inca people defeated an enemy, they absorbed its land into its empire. An Inca noble would be sent to the territory to rule, while the local leaders were allowed to remain in their positions, provided they showed loyalty to the Inca emperor. The children of the conquered enemy were sent to the Inca capital city of Cuzco, where they were taught Inca ways before being returned to their homes. All the conquered people had to work for the Inca, and pay tribute, or "mit'a". This was a form of taxation usually paid by working on one of the Inca's projects. Men may have served in the army, worked in mines or quarries, or been assigned to build and maintain a vast network of roads and bridges that linked all corners of the Inca Empire. They also had to give up part of their land to grow crops for the empire. The advantage of this was that surplus grain was sent to either religious or imperial storehouses. The religious storehouses fed the priests and provided offerings to the gods. The imperial storehouses not only fed the noblemen, state officials, and craftsmen, but also provided food for those who were too sick or elderly to work in the fields. In some ways, this system was an early example of a welfare state.

Governing the Inca Empire

The Inca Empire was notable for its high level of organization. The empire was organized in the form of a social pyramid. At the top of the pyramid was the Sapa Inca, or emperor. The

Inca weavers have been renowned for their textiles for centuries: Many traditional designs are still made today and worn by the Inca's descendants. Each design is specific to the particular village from which it comes.

ca believed that the emperor was descended
om the sun and, as a consequence, he
as treated as a god. He had absolute
ower. After the emperor died, his body was
eserved in his palace and his servants
ntinued to wait on him. One of the main
stivals held in Cuzco was the procession of
e mummies of long-dead Sapa Incas through
e city streets.

Below the Sapa Inca in the hierarchy of
ca society were the four governors, who each
led one of the four quarters of the empire.
ach quarter was sub-divided into provinces,
nd the governors of each of these provinces
ere under the command of the four main
overnors. Beneath the provincial governors
me the local rulers and leaders.

At the bottom of Inca society, and making
p the majority of the empire, were the ordinary
eople, who were mostly farmers. Their lives
ere highly controlled, to the extent that they
ere not permitted to travel without official
uthorization, and they were not even allowed
own luxury goods, such as gold and silver
bjects, which were strictly reserved for
ossession by the nobility only.

The Inca Empire 1200–1532 CE

1200 CE According to Inca legend, the first Inca ruler, Manco Capac,
came to power and founded the city of Cuzco.

1438–1463 CE Emperor Pachacuti extends the Inca Empire from Lake
Titicaca in the southeast to Lake Junín in the northwest.

1463–1471 CE Topa Inca, Pachacuti's son, extends the empire along
the north coast of Peru.

1471–1493 CE Emperor Topa Inca extends the empire south to Chile.

1493–1525 CE Emperor Huayna Capac further extends the empire as
far north as Colombia.

1525 CE News of white men in Panama reaches the Inca.

1532 CE Spanish defeat the Inca. Emperor Atahualpa killed.

*The Inca called their empire Tahuantinsuyu,
meaning "Land of the Four Quarters." The
quarters were: Chinchasuyu in the north;
Cuntisuyu in the west; Antisuyu in the east;
and Collasuyu in the south. At the center lay
Cuzco, the Inca capital. To control their vast
empire, the Inca built a great network of
roads, often over difficult mountain terrain.*

Inca Sites

Cuzco

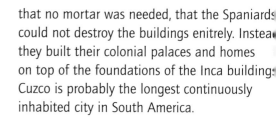

The capital city of the Inca, Cuzco, was at the heart of the Inca Empire. The city dates from around 1200 CE, but in its early days it was little more than a collection of wooden and thatch houses. In the 15th century CE its fortunes changed when the Inca emperor Pachacuti rebuilt the city in stone.

Cuzco also lay at the physical heart of the four quarters of the empire. All the roads built by the Incas to link the many Inca towns and villages started at Cuzco. The four quarters into which the empire was split were marked from the main square in Cuzco, the Huacacapata. The city was laid out in the shape of a puma, which was a sacred animal to the Inca. Each of the governors of the four quarters was required to live for a part of the year in Cuzco. He lived in the quarter of the city that corresponded to the quarter of the empire he governed.

The emperor's palace was the seat of government and it was from here that the empire was ruled. The most sacred of all the whole Inca shrines was the "Temple of the Sun." The temple contained statues of the gods, and other sacred goods were also stored there. The walls were covered with beautiful tapestries. Only priests and very important people were allowed to enter the temple. Most of the ceremonies were held outside in the main square.

When the Spanish conquerors arrived in Cuzco, they were amazed at the wealth they saw. After they removed the gold and silver, they set about destroying the city. However, the Incas had built their structures so well from large blocks of stone, cut to fit together so precisely that no mortar was needed, that the Spaniards could not destroy the buildings enitrely. Instead they built their colonial palaces and homes on top of the foundations of the Inca buildings. Cuzco is probably the longest continuously inhabited city in South America.

Machu Picchu

Hidden from the world for centuries until the ruins were rediscovered in 1911 CE by Hiram Bingham, a U.S. historian, the ruins of Machu Picchu continue to puzzle archeologists. Although it is clear that farming was practised at Machu Picchu, archaeologists are not sure of the city's function. They think it was most likely a sacred site, because of the alignment of the sun and some of the structures built there.

The ruins occupy one of the world's most spectacular locations, approximately 43 miles (70 km) northwest of Cuzco, The Machu Picchu complex was built on a steep rocky ridge, at an elevation of 2,000 feet (600 m), surrounded by high mountains. On either side of the ridge, the mountainsides fall away steeply to the valley of the sacred Urubamba River. The city can only be

Buildings in Cuzco, Peru, still stand on foundations built by the Inca some 800 years ago. Although the walls were built without any cement or mortar, the blocks fit so closely together that it is impossible to slide a sheet of paper between them. Over the centuries, they have withstood a number of serious earthquakes.

en from one side, from the mountain road
1 the south. From the river valley, it is invisible,
hich might help to explain why Machu Picchu
as never attacked and why it remained
ndiscovered for so many centuries.

Mountain Farmers

here are almost 300 buildings, all constructed
om stone, within Machu Picchu. They are
rincipally arranged along the sides of a large
blong plaza. There are a series of one-roomed
ouses, each was probably occupied by a single
amily. The role of other, special structures
emains uncertain, but was probably linked to
eligious rituals. Despite the extremely
nhospitable terrain, the inhabitants of Machu
Picchu transformed the steep mountainsides
nto terraces on which they grew crops. A stone
aqueduct was constructed to supply fresh water
from the mountain streams. The water was
conducted throughout the city via a series of
channels and basins. It was also fed to the
farming terraces on the lower slopes.

Stone Builders

The Inca people were highly skilled architects,
engineers, and stonemasons. Machu Picchu
represents the highest point of their skills
as builders, because the site they chose was
extremely difficult to access. All their materials
had to be carried up to the ridge. The builders
used tools, such as stone and bronze chisels,
hammers, and crowbars. The large blocks of
stones were shaped into single pieces using
hammers. The blocks often had rounded edges
or were polished so that the stone caught the
sunlight and created patterns.

The stonemasons were so skilled that they
fitted the blocks together without needing to
use mortar. While the different buildings lost
their thatched roofs long ago, the walls were so
well constructed that they have withstood the
many earthquakes that have hit the Andean
region ever since they were built.

This photographic view of Machu Picchu in present-day Peru shows its dramatic mountain setting, and the masterful way in which the Inca builders utilized the natural contours of the site. Because of its isolated location, Machu Picchu remained undiscovered for centuries after it was abandoned by the Inca.

GLOSSARY

adobe Sun-dried mud-bricks, used for building houses.

agave A type of cactus. It was used as a food and to make an alcoholic drink.

cactus A prickly desert plant, characterized by large, tough stems, brightly colored flowers, and leaves reduced to spines or scales.

chinampa A small plot of land reclaimed from the mud of lakes in Central Mexico. The plots were used for growing crops.

conquistadores A Spanish word for "conquerors." It is usually applied to the Spanish conquerors of Mexico and Peru in the 16th century.

copal A hard aromatic yellow, orange, or red resin from various tropical trees. It was used in varnishes as well as for incense.

gorget A breast ornament of stone, shell, or metal with holes for wearing on a cord around the neck.

hunters and gatherers People who live by hunting animals and gathering wild plants for food.

Ice Age A period of cold climate when much of Earth's surface was covered with ice. There were, in fact, several Ice Ages. The last one began about 70,000 years ago and ended only about 10,000 years ago.

Inuit (Eskimo) The inhabitants of the Arctic coasts and islands. There are two main groups: the Yupik who inhabit eastern Siberia and southern and central Alaska, and the Inuit who stretch from northern Alaska to Greenland. In Canada Inuit (meaning "people") has come to replace "Eskimo," the name given by neighboring Native Americans and later adopted by Europeans.

Iroquois A term usually restricted to the Native American groups who allied to form the League of the Iroquois in the 16th century: the Seneca, Cayuga, Onondaga, Oneida, Mohawk, and Tuscarora.

Iroquoian A term referring to all Native American groups speaking Iroquoian languages.

litter A vehicle in the form of a chair or couch carried on poles on people's shoulders.

mesquite A thorny shrub bearing edible beanlike pods. It grows in Mexico and the southwestern United States.

mestizo The name given in Latin America to a person of mixed Native American and European descent.

mica A mineral-bearing rock that can be split into thin transparent sheets.

mummy The remains of a dead person preserved in accordance with traditional religious belief.

native A local inhabitant of a country. In America the term refers to the American Indians. Today many American Indians prefer to be called Native Americans.

nomadic The term used to describe those who wander from place to place, usually in search of food.

Norse The people of ancient Scandinavia, especially Norway.

prehistoric The term used to describe the period in history before the appearance of written records. In American Indian history this is usually taken to mean before 1492 (the year Columbus arrived).

quetzal bird A Central American bird of the pheasant family, prized for its brightly colored feathers.

sarcophagus A stone coffin, often decorated with sculpture or carving.

semidesert Land that is very dry but where it is still possible for some plants to grow for part of the year at least.

stirrup-spout A hollow handle and spout in the shape of a stirrup (a horserider's footrest). A typical feature of Moche pottery.

supernatural Beyond the ordinary forces of nature, to do with gods and other mysterious beings.

travois A wheelless vehicle used by the Plains Indians of North America to carry their belongings, consisting of a V-shaped framework of poles fastened to an animal's back and dragged along the ground behind it. It was pulled by dogs and (after about 1700) by horses.

UBLICATIONS

tecs: Reign of Blood and Splendor. Time-Life Books, 1992.

quedano, Elizabeth. Aztec, Inca, and Maya. Dorling Kindersley, 993.

e, Michael D. The Maya. Thames and Hudson, 2005.

e, Michael D. Mexico: From the Olmecs to the Aztecs. Thames and Hudson, 2002.

oke, Tim. Ancient Aztec (National Geographic Investigates). National Geographic, 2007.

by, Anita. Ancient Pueblo (National Geographic Investigates). National Geographic, 2007.

obon, Guy E. Archaeology of Prehistoric Native America: An Encyclopedia. Routledge, 1998.

rris, Nathaniel. Ancient Maya (National Geographic Investigates). National Geographic, 2008.

acs, Sally Senzell. Picture the Past: Life in a Hopi Village. Heinemann Library, 2001.

rson, Timothy. Anasazi (Ancient Civilizations), Steadwell Books, 2001.

und Builders and Cliff Dwellers. Time-Life Books, 1992.

rl, Lila. Ancient Maya (People of the Ancient World). Franklin Watts, 2005.

Lawrence, Genevieve. The Pueblo and their History (We the People). Compass Point Books, 2005.

arer, Robert, and Loa Traxler. The Ancient Maya. Stanford University Press, 2005.

ith, Michael E. The Aztecs (Peoples of America). Blackwell, 2002.

nneborn, Liz. The Ancient Aztecs (People of the Ancient World). Franklin Watts, 2005.

uart, George E. Ancient Pioneers: The First Americans. National Geographic, 2001.

e Magnificent Maya (Lost Civilizations series). Time-Life Books, 993.

WEB SITES

http://dallasmuseumofart.org/dig/maya/index.htm
Dig! The Dallas Museum of Art Maya Project.

http://www.archaeology.org/interactive/belize/index.html
Follow an interactive dig at a Mayan site in Belize.

http://historylink101.com/1/mayan/ancient_mayan.htm
Historylink page with information about all aspects of Maya life.

http://library.thinkquest.org/27981/
ThinkQuest Aztec site.

http://archaeology.la.asu.edu/tm/index2.php
The Templo Mayor Museum of Aztec history in Mexico City.

http://www.public.asu.edu/~mesmith9/
Homepage and blog of Aztec archaeologist Michael E. Smith.